Everyday Nature Secrets

DISCOVER THE HIDDEN WORLD IN YOUR BACKYARD

CONTENTS

A Birds & Blooms Book

© 2023 RDA Enthusiast Brands, LLC

1610 N. 2nd St., Suite 102
Milwaukee, WI 53212-3906

Illustrations throughout
Katy Dockrill (drawings); Getty Images: Angelina Bambina; Ganna Galata; Liubov Khutter-Kukkonin; Oksana Latysheva; Filo; Marabird; Maria_Galybina; Marylia Design; Utro_na_more (accent shapes)

Front cover photo credits
Getty Images: Bernard Lynch (butterfly); Michael Clay Smith (bird); Marcia Straub (nest); Westend61 (plant)

Back cover photo credits
Richard Day/Daybreak Imagery (butterfly); Getty Images: GummyBone (bird); RyanJLane (tomatoes)

ISBN
978-1-62145-907-1

Component Number
119500104S

We are committed to both the quality of our products and the service we provide to our customers. We value your comments, so please feel free to contact us at *TMBBookTeam@ TrustedMediaBrands.com*.

For more Birds & Blooms products and information, visit our website: *www.birdsandblooms.com*

Text, photography and illustrations for *Everyday Nature Secrets* are based on articles previously published in *Birds & Blooms*, *Country*, *Country Woman*, *Reader's Digest* and *Our Canada* magazines.

Printed in China
10 9 8 7 6 5 4 3 2 1

ANNA MORRISON

Nature at Your Doorstep

Open the door—what do you see? If Mother Nature has anything to say about the matter, there are sure to be a few surprises in store. Today, a camera-shy bird might finally fly down from the canopy, enticed by a bubbling birdbath. Or maybe the tomatoes will be ripe at last (just don't let the squirrels know).

This book is designed to lead you on an adventure through your own backyard by exploring familiar flowers, fliers and flutterers from intriguing new perspectives. What kinds of visitors stop by your garden when the sun goes down? How can a love of nature build stronger and happier communities? Why do ladybugs have spots? Read on to find out—and always remember to invite nature into your life.

—The editors of
***Birds & Blooms* magazine**

CHAPTER 1

Nature at Night

AN INKY SKY AND STARLIGHT SET THE STAGE FOR AN EVENING MAGIC SHOW. WHAT TRICKS DOES MOTHER NATURE HAVE UP HER SLEEVE?

As the sun goes down, a new world of natural activity awakens. Owls soar silently through the night sky; moths flutter among silvery white blooms that glisten in the moonlight; and the black-crowned night heron stands stock-still at the water's edge, waiting for a midnight snack to swim or scuttle within reach. Take an evening stroll with us through this twilight paradise, and get ready to unravel the mysteries of nature at night.

MEET YOUR NOCTURNAL NEIGHBORS

Owls are widespread, yet they tend to keep a low profile. Let's shed some light on the most common varieties in North America.

Burrowing owls. An oddity in the owl world, burrowing owls are among the few types to nest underground. The southern Florida populations dig their own chambers, while those in the Southwest rely on holes dug by other animals. Look for these petite owls perched on fence posts or other low perches, swiveling their heads from side to side.

▶ **BARN OWLS**
True to their name, barn owls tend to nest and roost in barns, silos and other human-made structures. These skilled rodent-slayers have heart-shaped faces and are ghostly white, with warm brown coloration on their backs and wings. The North American barn owl is the largest of the more than 40 barn owl races found worldwide.

▲ BARRED OWLS

Who cooks for you? Who cooks for you allll? This is the eerie-sounding call of the barred owl, heard throughout forests in the eastern United States, southern Canada and, increasingly, the Pacific Northwest. The expansion of barred owls into Washington and Oregon is a threat to spotted owls, because the larger and more aggressive barred owls displace the spotted species. Yet barred owls have a threat of their own to fear: Nearby great horned owls are among their major predators.

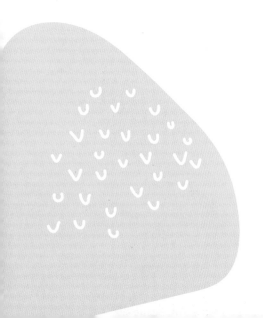

▼ SCREECH-OWLS

There are three species of screech-owls in the United
States: eastern in the East, western in the West, and
whiskered along the southern borders of Arizona and
New Mexico. Location aside, one of the best ways to
distinguish between them is by their calls. Eastern
screech-owls can be heard giving their best whinnying
horse impersonations. Western and whiskered
screech-owls call out with hoots, toots and doots.

▲ SHORT-EARED OWLS

Short-eared owls live in open areas, preferring to hunt and roost in grasslands, marshes and tundra. As you might have guessed from their name, their "ears" are so short, they are difficult to see at all. Short-eared owls are also one of the few owl species to build their own nests. The female scrapes a bowl-shaped nest into the ground and lines it with materials like grass and soft feathers.

Long-eared owls. These owls, slim doppelgängers of the great horned species, don't typically construct their own nests, instead moving into abandoned ones built by other birds such as crows and hawks. Long-eareds roost in thick foliage near open areas, where they hunt for voles, mice and rabbits.

▶ GREAT HORNED OWLS

The great horned is one of the most widespread owl species in North America. These tough birds are able to take down other large predators such as ospreys and falcons with their strong talons. Their diverse diet can include porcupines, scorpions, bats, skunks and even other owls. Despite their name, these birds don't actually have horns— the two telltale points at the tops of their heads are feather tufts.

SUNSET BIRDING

You don't have to be up at dawn to enjoy bird-watching. Look and listen for these intriguing fliers in the evening glow.

Nightjars. Members of this nocturnal group have ridiculously wide mouths, which they use to scoop flying insects right out of the air. They're sometimes referred to as goatsuckers, based on a myth that they come out at night to nurse from goats. Many, such as the eastern whip-poor-will and chuck-will's-widow, are named after their loud and repetitive calls.

◄ NIGHTHAWKS

One nightjar of note is the common nighthawk, which sports long, slender wings and has a seemingly erratic flight pattern. True to their name, nighthawks are most active at night, though you can occasionally see them foraging during the day. You'll be alerted to their presence by a *pzeent* call that sounds similar to that of a woodcock.

▲ CHIMNEY SWIFTS

Historically, chimney swifts would roost in hollow trees, in caves and along cliffs, but these days they are almost entirely dependent on human structures for their nighttime needs. After soaring around all day searching for flying insects, swifts congregate in communal roosts, often in smokestacks and chimneys. You can watch as thousands of them fly into such structures at dusk, most notably during migration. In recent years, the chimney swift has been declining as these open roosting sites become less common. In some instances, artificial chimney swift towers have been installed to help the population.

◀ WILSON'S SNIPES

These shorebirds make impressive aerial displays as the sun goes down. High circles and shallow dives are accompanied by a hollow, haunting sound known as winnowing, which is created by air flowing over the bird's tail. Look for Wilson's snipes in open wet areas, especially damp fields and marshy pond edges.

◀ WOODCOCKS

Woodcocks are portly shorebirds more at home in the upland woods than along the edge of the water. On spring evenings, males perform an elaborate territorial display in open areas adjacent to woods. They sit on the ground making a repetitive *peent* call. Then they explode skyward. They circle higher and higher before plummeting back to the ground and repeating the entire process.

Bugs, Bats and Beyond

Birds aren't the only evening performers. These other animals can also be seen (and heard) taking part in sunset spectacles.

INSECTS
On steamy summer nights, you're likely to hear the chirps, ticks and throbs of tree crickets, true katydids, bush katydids and field crickets. The males of each species woo females by rubbing their raspy legs against their body or scraping one wing against the other.

BATS
Bats can be seen fluttering in the twilight hours as they feed on insects. For your best chance at spotting them, try looking at city streetlights or over country ponds that offer a little glow.

FROGS AND TOADS
The American toad's trills and bullfrog's gulps may bring summer evenings to mind, but it takes only a few warm days early in the year to draw spring peepers and chorus frogs up from the mud, where they've slept all winter. Their loud songs can be heard a quarter mile away!

American robin

Owls. Sunset is a great time to go on an owl walk. In many areas you can hear owls throughout the year, but late winter is an especially active period, since it's breeding season for several species. Late summer, when bold little owlets start testing their vocal chords, is also a treat. Keep in mind: Not all owls hoot! Some species trill, wail or whinny.

▲ SONGBIRDS

While not as boisterous as the sunrise chorus, there is a flurry of songbird activity as the day turns to night. Robins, mockingbirds and many other daylight-loving birds belt out tunes at night for the same reasons they do so during the day: to establish their territories and attract mates. Noise pollution from humans lessens after dark, so the songs of birds are not drowned out.

BAT MYTHS, BUSTED

If the mere thought of a bat makes you shiver, read on—the truths behind these common bat myths might change your mind.

MYTH:

Most bats have rabies.

REALITY:

According to the United States Humane Society, less than half of 1% of all bats in the United States carry rabies. In the entire country, bats cause only 1.3 cases of human rabies per year. And while you should always exercise caution with respect to wildlife, more people die annually from lightning strikes than they do from rabies in the United States.

MYTH:

Bats are ugly, gangly and graceless.

REALITY:

Bats are graceful aerial acrobats. They are the only mammal that truly flies, and they often put on a great show with high-speed twists and turns, using an echolocation system so advanced we have yet to fully understand how it works.

MYTH:

**Bats want to suck
your blood.**

REALITY:

No vampire bats live in
the U.S., so you needn't
worry about a backyard
visitor looking for his next
meal. And vampire bats
don't like human blood
anyway—they prefer
that of farm animals.

MYTH:

**Bats are aggressive
toward humans.**

REALITY:

Bats don't attack humans.
If they swoop close, they're
probably chasing after one
of the tasty mosquitoes
or gnats swirling around
our heads.

Biggest Bat Benefits

**Bats aren't the bad guys. Here's why
they're more helpful than you think!**

- Like bees, bats are important
  pollinators. They pollinate
  more than 300 varieties of
  fruit, including mangoes and
  bananas, as well as almond
  and cashew trees.
- In the tropics, fruit-eating bats
  are critical to seed dispersal
  and forest regeneration.
- Bat droppings, called guano, are
  a very effective fertilizer. When
  collected responsibly, guano
  can have a very positive effect
  on local economies. And if you
  like tequila, thank bats! They
  help fertilize agave, tequila's
  main ingredient.
- Bats can eat close to their
  weight in insects every night—
  more than 1,000 mosquitoes
  in an hour. Bats also consume
  huge quantities of agricultural
  pests, reducing the need for
  toxic pesticides.

BAT HOUSE ESSENTIALS

Like many birds, bats can thrive in human-made houses. Here's what you need to know to make these nighttime fliers feel at home.

▶ **SET THE SCENE**

It's important to install a bat house in a place where bats are protected and have access to vital resources. A spot with sun exposure that's close to water and a mix of farmland and natural areas is ideal. Mount the house on a tall pole and add a metal predator guard for extra security.

Mount the house at least 12 feet off the ground— higher is better.

Large boxes, more than 2 feet tall and 14 inches wide, are key to housing colonies.

Well-sealed houses keep bats dry and happy.

Vents provide air circulation for the colony.

The warmer the climate you live in, the lighter the bat house should be painted or stained to keep the bats cool.

Look for an entrance at the bottom.

Wood, fiber cement and plastic are acceptable building materials.

WOODLINK.

NORTH AMERICAN BATS TO KNOW

More than 1,400 bat species have been identified worldwide. These common North American bats stand out from the crowd.

▶ MEXICAN FREE-TAILED BAT

Bats wing through the air on thin membranes stretched between their elongated "fingers." A smaller membrane usually connects the hind limbs and spans the tail, which extends well beyond the membrane in these migratory bats. Mexican free-tails are usually found in large cave colonies, but they will also roost in houses and buildings.

Silver-haired bat. Although most North American bats give birth to a single baby, this species produces twins. Bats give birth while hanging at their roosts, then nurse their offspring for several weeks. Young ones cling to their mothers' bellies until they can fly independently.

Little brown bat. Probably the most abundant bat in North America, this species is common in and around cities. On summer days, thousands may hang upside down in an attic or loft. These sleeping groups are composed solely of females and young. Males also roost during the day but usually as solitary individuals.

▲ BIG BROWN BAT

Occasionally seen flying during the day, big brown bats usually emerge at twilight to pursue prey over meadows, suburban streets and city traffic. They detect beetles and other insects by emitting high-pitched sounds that bounce off objects and come back as echoes. The same technique, known as echolocation and used by other insect-eating bats, also helps them avoid obstacles.

"*I often think that the night is more alive and more richly colored than the day.*"

—VINCENT VAN GOGH

Screech-owl

SPOTLIGHT ON MOTHS

In a world of bright butterflies, don't forget about these fascinatingly cool insects.

When it comes to an insect popularity contest between butterflies and moths, butterflies tend to get most of the attention. Butterflies are often, but not always, larger and more colorful. Plus, most moth species usually fly at night, when we're not as likely to see them. But this isn't a reason to ignore moths. Some species are important pollinators, and all are a great food source for birds and other wildlife you want to attract. To attract moths, plant their caterpillar host plants and don't spray pesticides.

▶ ISABELLA TIGER MOTH

Common across North America, you're most likely to encounter this moth in its caterpillar phase, when it's known as a woolly bear. These furry caterpillars sport reddish brown and black bands and are often spotted on the move in the fall. Attract them with asters, birches, elms and maples, and by leaving fallen leaves in your garden. They emerge in the spring as pretty, medium-sized, pale yellow moths; adult females boast orange hindwings.

Woolly bear

▲ IO MOTH

This large, widespread moth has a wingspan of more than 4 inches. Males have pale yellow forewings, and females have reddish brown. Both males and females have a striking "eyespot" on each hindwing, which helps deter predators. Host plants include hackberry, willow, mesquite, redbud, currant and blackberry.

◀ ROYAL WALNUT MOTH

This giant has a wingspan of more than 6 inches, with the females larger than the males. The upper sides of its wings are reddish brown with random pale yellow spots. It's found from the Midwest to the Atlantic and Gulf coasts. As its name suggests, walnut is its caterpillar host plant, along with hickory, pecan, butternut, sweet gum, persimmon and sumac. The caterpillars, known as hickory horned devils, are 5-inch green giants with orange horns.

▼ ROSY MAPLE MOTH

It doesn't get prettier than this species, with its pale pink and yellow color scheme. This moth is found over much of eastern North America, from southern Canada down to Florida and East Texas. Its caterpillars feed on the leaves of maples and oaks.

▲ SCARLET-BODIED WASP MOTH

This gorgeous moth has a bright red body with black-lined, clear wings. You might have trouble believing it's a moth at all, because it looks more like a wasp. This mimicry behavior helps keep the moth's predators at bay. It's found in coastal areas from South Carolina through Florida and across the Gulf Coast into Texas. Hemp vine is its caterpillar host plant.

Moth or Butterfly?

Use these general tips to help differentiate between the two.

MOTH

- Thick, furry body
- Threadlike or frondlike antennae
- When resting, wings fold down over the body so wing tops are visible.

BUTTERFLY

- Thin, smooth body
- Smooth antennae ending in a bulb or "club"
- When resting, wings fold up over the body so undersides are visible.

MOON GARDEN MAGIC

Most people love to linger in gardens during the daytime, with sunlight splashing across colorful blooms. But a little planning can make your garden just as inviting by moonlight.

Woolly lambs' ears

◄ LUMINOUS LEAVES

Bright leaves show up well at night. Among those that especially seem to glow in the pale moonlight are plants with variegated or gold- or silver-tinged foliage. Try planting Russian sage, lavender, woolly lambs' ears, sea kale, santolina or horned poppy.

Look for plants that are described as flowering at dusk, opening in late afternoon, blooming in the evening or night blooming. They'll all provide open flowers well into the evening, and some will go throughout the night. Such plants might include evening primrose, moonflower, four o'clocks, yucca, and Moon Frolic and Toltec Sundial daylilies.

Lavender

◄ PRETTY PASTELS
Pastel blooms in shades of pale pink, yellow, blue or lavender reflect the light of the moon and stars, giving your garden a delicate glow and often appearing to shimmer at twilight. Good choices include lavender and passionflower.

White flowers offer classic beauty and become especially important when the sun goes down. A single white blossom here or there can be easily lost in the dark, but a mass of them will light up your garden. Stagger bloom times to enjoy a full season of showy white flowers.

Night pollinators, including moths, native bees and bats, are attracted to white and pale-colored flowers that are intensely fragrant and produce a lot of nectar. Plants with flowers that stay open through the night, such as yucca, or blossoms that open at dusk and close in the morning, such as evening primrose, are magnets for these industrious third-shift pollinators.

Many night-loving plants release fragrance that's the most spicy, intoxicating, or intense in early evening or at night. Consider lilac, mock orange, fragrant columbine, flowering tobacco and night phlox.

A moon garden is designed to be enjoyed without a flood of artificial light. Choose white or pale benches, stepping stones and accessories—not just for aesthetics but also for safety.

– Field Notes –

Pretty in Pink

Cactuses bloom here in Arizona each spring, but this night-blooming Argentine giant I saw in Fountain Hills is pretty rare. The great majority of this species' blooms are white instead of pink. This particular bloom caught my eye one early morning as I was on my way to the store. I was very lucky because the flowers stay open for about six hours before wilting in the late morning. I quickly went home to grab my Nikon D750 and 50 mm lens. I got the shot I wanted!

—Spencer Fairbanks
Fountain Hills, Arizona

10 MIDNIGHT-HUED BLOOMS

While light-colored flowers and foliage dazzle under the moonlight, these darker blooms bring nighttime mystery into the light.

1 ◄ DARK AND HANDSOME HELLEBORE

Helleborus 'Dark and Handsome', Zones 4 to 9. Dark and Handsome steals your heart with black-purple good looks. This sturdy chap stands its ground when facing ravaging deer and rabbits, and it quickly naturalizes in woodland gardens. Hellebores thrive in part to full shade; after the blooms fade, attractive leathery green foliage remains.

2 Chocolate Cosmos

Cosmos atrosanguineus, Zones 9 to 11 or Annual. Chocolate cosmos sprout from tender tubers that can be grown as annuals or brought inside for winter in cold climates. Ultimately reaching up to 30 inches tall, they shine from midsummer into fall and are easy to care for.

3 Black Barlow Columbine

Aquilegia vulgaris 'Black Barlow', Zones 3 to 9. This deep maroon, almost black double-petaled columbine adds drama to a late spring garden. Grow this 24- to 30-inch perennial in sun or part shade. It's short-lived, but it may rebloom if it's deadheaded, and it self-sows like a champ.

4 Black Knight Hollyhock

Alcea rosea 'Black Knight', Zones 4 to 9. Black Knight scores with deep purple-black blooms even in its first year. If planted in full sun, this 5- to 6-foot-tall butterfly and hummingbird magnet will readily self-sow. It also grows within range of troublesome black walnut tree roots and resists rust.

5 Black Iris

Iris chrysographes, Zones 4 to 8. It's hard to find a true black flower, but this iris is very close. Grow it in sun to part shade among perennials with rounded leaves so its spiky plumes peek out of the mounds. Irises attract butterflies and hummingbirds, and they make lovely, velvety dark cut flowers.

6 ▲ PERSIAN LILY

Fritillaria persica, Zones 4 to 8. Persian lilies have been around since 1573 but are still not widely planted. They provide architectural intensity to a spring garden, with 20 to 30 dark plum, bell-shaped blooms lining up in alternating rows on slender stalks.

7 Halloween Improved Pansy
Viola x *wittrockiana* 'Halloween Improved', **Zones 6 to 8.** This black pansy is all treat, no trick. A step up from a pansy named Halloween II, Halloween Improved has fewer white stripes and more blooms than its predecessor. It's spookily festive when paired with orange pansies.

8 Black Satin Dahlia
Dahlia 'Black Satin', **Zones 8 to 11.** Growing 4 to 6 feet tall, this formal decorative dahlia produces large pompon flowers. The chocolaty poufs are edged with a deep burgundy flare. One of the biggest perks is that the more flowers you cut, the more flowers you will get.

9 Crazytunia Black Mamba
Petunia hybrida 'Crazytunia Black Mamba', **Zones 9 to 11 or Annual.** Velvety and dark, these are considered the best almost-black petunias you can grow. Plant them in full sun for the best bloom power. Hummingbirds love them, and there's no deadheading needed! The old flowers drop off as they start to wilt.

10 ▼ QUEEN OF NIGHT TULIP
Tulipa 'Queen of Night', **Zones 3 to 8.** A favorite since the 1940s, Queen of Night is as mysterious as tulips get. The glistening deep maroon petals masquerade as black. Pair this queen with bright and cheery orange or pink tulips placed in well-draining soil in a sunny spot. Plant in fall for spring flowers.

Anna's
hummingbird

DEGREES OF HIBERNATION

Many animals make for warmer climates as temperatures drop. The rest hunker down. Here's how and where some of your favorite visitors snooze through the chilly weather.

◀ **BACKYARD BIRDS**
Birds generally don't hibernate, but chickadees, hummingbirds, doves and small owls have been known to go into a state of inactivity, called torpor, that lasts anywhere from a few hours to overnight. Favorite roosting spots for such birds include birdhouses, evergreens and tree cavities.

Only queen bumblebees survive the coldest months, while the rest of their colony dies. After mating with males and feeding on pollen, the fertilized queen leaves the nest to find a place to hibernate and live off her fat stores until spring.

Little brown bats stay inactive for more than six months in barns, hollow trees and attics, sometimes sheltering with other bats for warmth. Bats normally have incredibly speedy heart rates while flying—up to 1,000 beats per minute. While they hibernate, it can drop as low as 10 beats per minute.

▼ GROUNDHOGS

True hibernation champs, groundhogs hibernate inside burrows below the frost line in wooded or bushy areas for as long as 150 days. During that time, a groundhog's heart rate slows from 80 beats per minute to an amazing five beats per minute, and its body temperature falls from 99 degrees to as low as 33 degrees.

Mourning
cloak
butterfly

▲ BUTTERFLIES

Mourning cloaks, question marks, commas and some other butterflies winter as adults. Tucked away behind loose bark or in fallen leaves, they enter a state known as diapause, in which they dramatically slow their metabolism. Special chemicals in their bodies act as a natural antifreeze, and they remain dormant until warmer weather arrives.

Not all butterflies hibernate in an adult stage. Viceroys, also known as monarch look-alikes, employ an entirely different tactic. Caterpillars from the summer's last brood create shelters called hibernacula. The itty-bitty caterpillars instinctively know to chew a leaf in a specific pattern, then fold and fashion it into a tentlike structure. The rolled leaf is lined and fastened to a stalk with silk that the caterpillars spin themselves.

▼ SMALLER MAMMALS

Like some backyard birds, several mammals, including opossums, raccoons, skunks and chipmunks, enter a sort of mini-hibernation called torpor. They conserve energy for a short period, then wake to find food when temperatures rise and weather improves. Raccoons leave their dens in hollow trees, barns and crawl spaces to forage; chipmunks occasionally emerge from their underground burrows to retrieve food from hidden caches; and field mice leave their nests under tree stumps, rocks, decks or porches to nibble on nearby stores.

Raccoon

▲ REPTILES AND AMPHIBIANS

Unable to generate their own heat, cold-blooded critters such as frogs, turtles and salamanders survive frosty temperatures and scarce resources by slowing down considerably and often becoming inactive.

Some frogs and salamanders escape freezing temperatures by burrowing in the mud on the bottoms of ponds. Wood frogs and common box turtles burrow in leaves and actually freeze. Their bodies produce glucose, which acts like an antifreeze to protect their cells. Come spring, they thaw out and resume normal activity.

Backyard bugs preserve in various ways. Praying mantis eggs stay safe and cozy in insulated egg sacs. Most dragonflies in their wingless nymph stage survive the cold underwater. And if your house has ever been invaded by swarms of lady beetles or stinkbugs in fall, then you know their overwintering strategy all too well.

HIBERNATION BY THE NUMBERS

When it comes to sleep, why count sheep? Tally up these impressive hibernation facts from the animal kingdom instead.

10

Each autumn, some chipmunk species hoard food in underground burrows where they spend the winters. The pint-size critters create tunnels as long as 10 feet.

2.4

Common snapping turtles may travel as far as 2.4 miles to get to their preferred hibernation sites in shallow water. Once they're settled, their body temperature drops to 34 degrees.

55

Lady beetles are masters at fasting when temperatures drop. They live up to 9 months on stored reserves and eventually return to normal activity once it warms up to about 55 degrees.

3

Like many amphibians, American toads spend the winters burrowed as deep as 3 feet underground.

3,000

More than 3,000 species of solitary bees in the United States remain awake and somewhat active in winter, occupying hollow plant stems, abandoned beetle burrows, underground tunnels or dead standing trees.

1940

The common poorwill, a type of nightjar, enters a state of rest for days or weeks at a time. Scientists first discovered this behavior in the 1940s. It's one of the few birds known to hibernate.

27

The core body temperature of an Arctic ground squirrel may drop to 27 degrees during hibernation.

20

A hibernating bear's heart can stop for up to 20 seconds, and its respiration may fall to about a breath per minute.

2

Punxsutawney Phil is famous for emerging from his Pennsylvania den every Feb. 2, but many groundhogs, especially females, stay put until March, when warmer weather moves in.

ZZZ'S IN THE TREES: HOW BIRDS SLEEP

As night settles in, most birds that are active during the day find a secluded spot to catch some shut-eye. However, sleep in the avian world is often different than our rest.

▶ PERCHED FOR SHUT-EYE

The vast majority of songbirds are natural perchers. This holds true even while they rest. Chalk it up to a bird's physique: To hold up its body weight, a bird will instinctively tighten its tendons and clamp its feet onto a branch.

Do birds dream? While they're dozing, it's unclear if birds dream, although they can experience bouts of rapid eye movement. Research in zebra finches has shown that brain neurons associated with song can be activated during sleep, yet this could simply be a way of reinforcing song learning instead of proof of dreaming.

Young
chickadee

How long do birds sleep? Instead of getting prolonged rest, birds often take hundreds of short snoozes each day. In a variety of instances, birds are never really asleep—at least not in the way that people think. Half of a bird's brain stays active while it is resting due to a phenomenon called unihemispheric slow-wave sleep. This helps birds detect potential predators and adjust to changing environmental conditions.

Hummingbirds are the ultimate sleepers. During cold spells, hummingbirds lower their metabolism and body temperature. They enter an overnight state called torpor, which almost mimics hibernation in other animals.

▲ NEST GUESTS

Birds rarely use nests as night roosts when they aren't incubating eggs or babies, but some cavity nesters, like wrens, take to nest boxes throughout the year. Others, such as bluebirds and pygmy nuthatches, have been documented roosting with small groups.

What do sleeping birds do to stay warm? Maintaining warmth is a challenge for sleeping birds. Feathers provide strong insulation, so birds tuck into themselves. As they snooze, ducks, geese and swans are often seen with their bills buried in their own feathers. Many species will also pull a leg up into their cozy plumage.

Your Avian Sleep Questions, Answered

Experts Kenn and Kimberly Kaufman explain nighttime bird sounds and the quirky sleeping habits of some woodpeckers.

Q Do birds snore? I hear birds outside my window and wonder if the sound I hear is snoring.
—*Mae Miller*
Marengo, Iowa

KENN AND KIMBERLY: That's an interesting question! Snoring isn't normal behavior for most birds, although it's reported that some large birds at times make audible breathing sounds when they're asleep. In general, birds are silent when they're sleeping. Birds that roost together in large flocks, such as starlings or blackbirds, may be somewhat noisy all night, but we assume that those are individuals waking up momentarily, calling out and then going back to sleep. But that doesn't usually happen when it's just a few birds. So we're not sure what you're hearing outside your window. Could it be some other kind of creature? Some crickets, frogs, toads, etc., have very birdlike voices.

Q I spotted a downy woodpecker on the side of my sugar maple tree. It had its head turned and tucked into its wings as if it was sleeping. What was it doing?
—*Larry Barger*
Hamilton, Ohio

KENN AND KIMBERLY: The bird you saw was likely taking a short nap. When downy woodpeckers go to sleep for the night, they usually escape to a tree cavity. But sometimes, even midday, a woodpecker may fall asleep for a short time while clinging to a tree trunk. It does this by bracing against the tree with stiff tail feathers and locking its toes onto the bark.

NATURAL GLOW: BRING MORE LIGHT TO YOUR NIGHT

Plenty of brightness can be found after sunset. Here are three great ways to see the light, even when it's dark out.

Look to the Stars

On summer nights, one of the easiest ways to enjoy nature is to head outside and look up. Marker Marshall, a ranger at Grand Canyon National Park, shares her quick tips for connecting constellations, identifying planets and partying with the stars.

Join the party. Stargazing alone can be a wonderful experience, but sharing the night with others can add a whole new dimension to your evening. Many national and state parks host star parties or festivals where guests can talk to pros and take advantage of telescopes and unhampered views. Grand Canyon National Park, where Marker works, throws an annual star party.

Master the basics. "Learn your constellations and they'll be like old friends helping you feel at home anywhere under dark, clear skies," Marker says. Download an app or find a star chart online at a site such as *skyandtelescope.com*. Once you know your zodiac constellations, it'll be easy to spot planets too. "Anytime you see a 'star' that doesn't belong in a constellation and isn't twinkling as much as it should be, you'll know you're seeing a planet," Marker says.

Mark your calendar. Plan ahead to catch the year's key celestial events—including meteor showers, lunar eclipses, supermoons, planetary movements and more. Certain events, such as the Perseid meteor shower, are visible around the same time every year.

Fire It Up

Whether you're looking to cozy up with a mug of hot cocoa or to enjoy some summertime s'mores on the beach, a bright, cheery bonfire is a great opportunity to spend time outside at night. Follow these tips to have your fire blazing bright in no time.

1. **Pick a spot.** Make sure the area is spacious, with no nearby buildings, and is free of debris and hazards such as trees and electrical cables.

2. **Gather tinder, kindling,** and small, medium and large logs. Hardwoods such as hickory or oak are best.

3. **Dig a wide,** shallow pit about 5 feet in diameter and 1 foot deep at the center of the circle.

4. **Start your blaze** small, with tight bundles of tinder (such as thin twigs and bark). Arrange the bundles in the center of the pit.

5. **Place the kindling** crosswise on top of the tinder. These should be twigs 8 to 10 inches long, slender enough to snap across your knee.

6. **Atop the kindling,** place the two smallest logs. Place two more atop them at right angles, creating a frame. Fill the space in the center with additional kindling.

7. **With longer logs,** form a tripod around the pile. Fill empty spaces with additional kindling.

8. **Keep adding logs** to the tripod, using longer pieces as you go, to create a tepee-like shape. Leave a space at the bottom so you can reach in with a long match and light the tinder.

9. **As the fire** burns, add more tinder, kindling and logs in the same fashion.

10. **Do not add** any products treated with salt, rubber, glue, plastic or foam to your bonfire. Do not use charcoal lighter fluid, aerosol products or combustible liquids to start your fire.

11. **When you leave,** cover embers with sand or dirt to properly extinguish the fire.

Plan ahead. Check nearby beaches and parks for after-hours or off-season availability. Review local ordinances for regulations—you may need a permit for a bonfire, even in your own backyard—and find out how far in advance you need to reserve a site.

Safety first. Have a water supply and fire extinguisher close by, just in case. Bring a flashlight, a cellphone (in case you have to dial 911), a shovel for covering the fire with sand or dirt, and a first-aid kit. Never leave a fire—even a smoldering one—unattended.

Catch Lightning in a Bottle

For many people, the first firefly sighting of the year conjures up fond childhood memories of running around the yard with an outstretched mason jar. While it's best to leave these luminescent insects free to roam and not cooped up in a makeshift lantern, adults and children alike can still enjoy their natural fireworks display. Here are some facts to ponder as you hunker down and look for the little shooting stars flitting about your backyard.

In Great Smoky Mountains National Park in Tennessee, one particular species of firefly *(photinus carolinus)* dazzles visitors with rippling displays of synchronized flashing.

Firefly light comes in three colors: yellow, orange and green.

Fireflies live as adults for about 21 days.

Fireflies aren't flies at all—they're actually a type of beetle.

Nearly 100% of the chemical reaction in a firefly's abdomen is released as light. They glow to find a mate, to communicate with members of their species and to show predators that they are distasteful.

"Adopt the pace
of nature:
Her secret is
patience."

—RALPH WALDO EMERSON

Burrowing
owl

On a Small Scale

A BIRD'S-EYE VIEW CAN SHOWCASE THE GRANDEUR OF NATURE, BUT SOME TINY TREASURES MERIT A MUCH CLOSER LOOK.

Peer into a flower bed and you're likely to discover a miniature world pulsing with life. Start down in the dark soil, where a skittering beetle is catching the light with its iridescent wing cases. Then let your gaze travel upward along a stem—will you spot a pollen-coated bumblebee reveling in a bloom's bounty, or a hovering hummingbird considering its next sip of nectar? Join us now on the ground level and explore the possibilities.

Silver-spotted skipper on zinnia

THE SECRET LIFE OF SKIPPERS

Small and speedy, skippers often fly under the radar, but they add lively interest to any garden.

◄ MOTH, BUTTERFLY OR SOMETHING ELSE?

Skippers belong to the order Lepidoptera, which includes all butterflies and moths. While they were once considered a third category within that order, most experts now agree that skippers are butterflies—a distinctive family known as the Hesperiidae.

What sets skippers apart? Skippers have stout bodies, big heads, and very rapid and erratic flight. They're smaller than the average butterfly, and most are not brightly colored. They tend to wear tones of brownish orange, black or gray.

Silver-spotted skipper caterpillar

Common sootywing on salvia

Are there many varieties? The United States and Canada have well over 200 species of skippers. As a result, identifying them can be a real challenge. Some people joke that they're called skippers because it is easier just to skip them! That said, it is simpler to separate the skippers into two major groups: spread-wings and grass skippers.

Spread-wing skippers usually sit with their wings stretched out to the sides or held above their backs (like most typical butterflies). Spread-wings are generally black, dark brown or gray, and they tend to have a wingspan of less than 2 inches.

ROLFNUSSBAUMER.COM

◄ COMMON CHECKERED-SKIPPER

This small spread-wing skipper sports bold black-and-white checkering that makes it easy to identify. Adults fly fast and low, often landing on the ground and visiting blooms such as clovers and marigolds.

The long-tailed skipper is common from Texas to Maryland. Long tails on the hindwings and a blue-green sheen on its body and wing bases make this spread-wing stand out. More migratory than most skippers, it sometimes wanders north, reaching as far as New England and the Great Lakes.

Attracting Skippers

Ready to roll out the welcome mat for skippers? Here's how.

WELCOME ADULT SKIPPERS
Flowers that attract other butterflies, such as coneflowers, asters and milkweeds, also attract adult skippers.

HOST SKIPPER CATERPILLARS
For spread-wing skipper caterpillars, plant as many native plants as possible. For grass skipper caterpillars, try researching the native grasses in your area.

AVOID INSECTICIDES
Insecticides kill skippers and other desirable pollinators! To make your yard more welcoming to these beneficial visitors, avoid using toxins.

Grass skippers are so named because their caterpillars use grasses as their host plants. Adults often adopt a posture called the jet-plane position, in which they hold their hindwings flattened out to the sides and their forewings raised above their heads. The jetlike shape is fitting—most grass skippers are amazingly fast fliers!

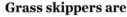

► **FIERY SKIPPER**
As native grasses have been crowded out in their habitat over time, fiery skippers have adapted to feed on Bermuda grass, a popular turf grass that was introduced to North America from Africa (not Bermuda) in the 1750s. Now abundant across the South, these grass skippers wander northward every year.

7 TINY BUTTERFLIES TO KNOW

Sure, these butterflies may be about the size of a thumbprint, but identifying and attracting them can be an oversized joy.

Dainty sulphur. Dainty sulphurs live up to their name! The smallest of the North American sulphurs, these petite fliers are found in open areas across most of the southern U.S. They have distinctive sulphur yellow underwings with three black dots. Their host plants include shepherd's needle, sneezeweed and cultivated marigold.

▶ **EASTERN TAILED-BLUE**
Tailed-blues stand out with beautiful black-edged azure wings and recognizable wing "tails." They flutter low to the ground and feed on smaller flowers because of their short proboscises. Their host plants include wild pea, yellow sweet clover and alfalfa.

Little metalmark. With a wingspan of just ½ to 1 inch, the little metalmark is the tiniest butterfly in this list. Its wings are rusty orange, with unique metallic streaks marking both sides. It's found in grassy areas along the Gulf Coast and the southeastern Atlantic region. Yellow thistle is its host plant.

American copper.
American coppers are widely distributed across the northern U.S. and southern Canada, often found along roadsides or in old fields. They are a tawny gray above with tigerlike black-spotted orange swathes, and they have silvery gray underwings flecked with black. Their host plants include sheep sorrel, mountain sorrel and curled dock.

▲ PEARL CRESCENT

The pearl crescent is part of the brushfoot family, which includes fritillaries and monarchs. Smaller than its cousins, with a wingspan of $1\frac{1}{4}$ to $1\frac{3}{4}$ inches, this orange and black-checked species is abundant from the East Coast to the Rockies. The males patrol open areas looking for females and sometimes dart out at intruders. Several species of asters are among their host plants.

Harvester. Orange and black on top with tawny spots on the underwings, this resident of eastern stream borders and swamps is no typical garden butterfly. Instead of nectar, adults sip aphid excretions, called honeydew. And the caterpillars are carnivorous—they eat aphids instead of plants.

LEFT: ROBERT KRAMER/GETTY IMAGES; RIGHT: RICHARD DAY/DAYBREAK IMAGERY

▼ GRAY HAIRSTREAK

The most common members of the hairstreak family, gray hairstreaks are slate gray above and soft gray underneath, with an orange spot near each hindwing tail. They also have white, black and orange streaks. Clover, cotton and mallow are their host plants.

Weighting Game

Just how much does a butterfly weigh?

Butterfly field guide author Paul Opler of Colorado State University estimates that a large swallowtail weighs 0.3 gram and smaller butterflies weigh 0.04 gram. The smallest, a pygmy-blue, would weigh only thousandths of a gram. For comparison, a single sugar cube weighs about 3 grams!

HOLY MACRO!

Through his camera lens, Russ Hayes of Sherbrooke, Quebec, captures a fascinating hidden world.

Honey bee

A few years ago, I bought a macro lens for my camera that allows me to capture extreme close-ups of my subjects. The purchase instantly changed my world of photography, opening up a whole new perspective on even ordinary objects. Raindrops on a clothesline, delicate spiderwebs and small feathers all become truly extraordinary under a macro lens.

Insects have become some of my favorite subjects to shoot. It takes a very steady hand, or a tripod, to manually focus on something so tiny; you can use autofocus, but when you are 4 to 8 inches away from a subject, the focus area is quite exacting. As with a human subject, I try to be sure that the insect's eyes are primarily in focus. This gets a little tricky since you don't want to scare away your bug while getting closer. Luckily, they sometimes seem mesmerized by the clicking noise of the shutter.

When I first started shooting with the macro lens, I was instantly amazed by how insects, including the common housefly, appeared up close. Sure, flies are gross, but they are also built like some sort of super

Snail

flying machine, with suction pads on their feet and alien-looking head parts. One of my first encounters was with the crane fly. It has extremely long legs and a head that somewhat resembles a horse's head because of its very long snout (called a rostrum). It also has defined knobs sticking out of the sides of its body. These are called halteres, which control the fly's bodily rotation in flight. This type of information was completely foreign to me before I began doing some online research about the species I was observing. Soon I was hooked! Every day I would scour the backyard vegetation for anything that moved, my camera at the ready.

Our neighbors wondered what I was always doing in our yard, so one day I put together a slideshow of about 200 close-up photos of various insects and added a soundtrack. I then invited the neighbors over to view the 20-minute show. Everyone was amazed. What excited me most was that they had no idea that these fascinating insects were a part of their everyday life but generally went unnoticed.

Developing a keen eye has brought some amazing, exciting photo ops my way: a monarch butterfly, so rare in Quebec now; the amazing color of the blue cuckoo wasp; fascinating ants tending their aphid farm (yes, they do milk the aphids); the unbelievable assassin or robber fly that catches other flies and prey in flight; the various families of spiders, including the tiny jumping spider, which is a cute little fur ball; countless

Ladybug larva

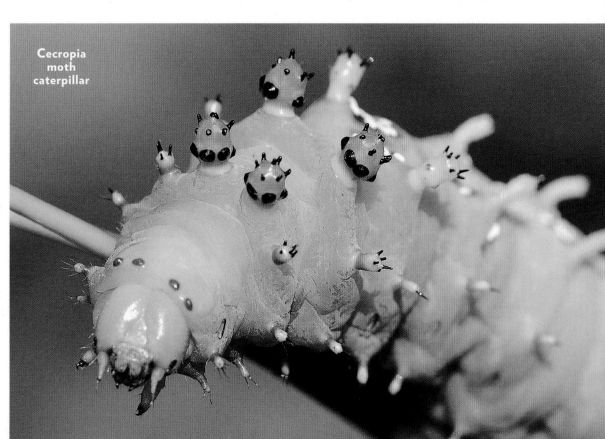

Cecropia moth caterpillar

Jumping
spider

butterflies and dragonflies—and so on! I share my favorite shots on my Facebook page, as I like to introduce my friends and family to the miniature world around us. In Canada, we get a respite from dealing with insects in winter, but they are a hardy bunch and always return, in one form or another, in spring. When they do, my camera and I are always waiting.

Cuckoo wasp

Ants farming aphids

MINIATURE MARVELS

These tiny plants can make a big impact on small-space gardens and containers.

◀ PIXIE DWARF ALBERTA SPRUCE
Picea glauca 'Pixie', **Zones 3 to 8.** This small spruce is a favorite among fairy gardeners. It has a natural conical shape— no pruning needed— and grows 1 to 2 inches per year. Its new growth is golden, as though it is sprinkled with fairy dust.

Bobo Hydrangea
Hydrangea paniculata 'Bobo', **Zones 3 to 8.** Award-winning Bobo is small in stature but big on blooms, which begin in midsummer and last up to 12 weeks. The dwarf plant's large creamy white flowers mature to a blush pink.

Soft Serve False Cypress
Chamaecyparis pisifera 'Dow Whiting', **Zones 5 to 7.** These diminutive evergreens are valued for their elegant stature and swirls of soft, touchable foliage. They can reach 6 to 10 feet but grow slowly, making them ideal for containers and rock gardens.

▼ LILAC CHIP BUTTERFLY BUSH

Buddleia 'Lilac Chip', Zones 5 to 9. Bees and butterflies love the long flower panicles of butterfly bush. Lilac Chip grows to about 2 feet and forms a mound of lavender-pink blooms that continue until frost.

Chiquita Coneflower

Echinacea 'Chiquita', Zones 4 to 10. Growing just 1 foot high, this sturdy, drought-resistant dwarf perennial pumps out large soft yellow flowers from July through September. The fragrant 3½-inch blooms attract bees and butterflies.

Dwarf Mondo Grass

Ophiopogon japonicus 'Nanus', Zones 6 to 11. This miniature, clumping grasslike plant grows 2 to 4 inches high and can be used as edging in flower beds or at the bases of statues and light fixtures. The slow-growing clumps are extremely low maintenance. If used as ground cover, they need to be mowed only once a year.

▲ MIGHTY MOUSE HOSTA

Hosta 'Mighty Mouse', **Zones 3 to 9.** Miniature hostas add texture and interest to rock gardens and troughs. This variegated cultivar has blue-green leaves with soft gold edges that age to cream. In early summer, the compact mound will be topped with tiny lavender blooms loved by bees.

▲ SHOW OFF SUGAR BABY FORSYTHIA

Forsythia x *intermedia* 'Show Off Sugar Baby', **Zones 4 to 9.** Sunny yellow forsythia flowers light up spring gardens, but many varieties mature into 8-foot giants. This tiny cultivar matures at just 30 inches. Its upright branches flower from base to tip, with more blooms per inch than any other cultivar.

Tiny Monster Geranium. *Geranium* 'Tiny Monster', **Zones 4 to 9.** This petite perennial makes an excellent low ground cover in sun or partial shade and can also be used in containers. Bright pink-magenta flowers emerge in late spring and are held above the tight mass of deep green leaves.

My Monet Weigela *Weigela Florida* 'My Monet', **Zones 4 to 6.** My Monet offers multiseason interest: Pink blooms attract hummingbirds in spring, and once the flowers fade, the cream, green and pink variegated foliage is showy till fall.

ZOOM IN ON MICROGREENS

Good things come in small packages when it comes to these nutrient-dense seedlings.

Radish microgreens

What are they? Microgreens are immature, near-perfect seedlings of your favorite vegetables and herbs—somewhere between sprouts and baby greens. Packed with flavor as well as nutrients, they often adorn plates at gourmet restaurants.

How do they taste? Delicate to intense, sweet to spicy, their flavors resemble those of the full-grown plant. Foodies and chefs love the myriad colors and textures too.

Why grow them yourself? Two words: instant gratification. You harvest these little guys when they're only 1½ to 2 inches tall, so they'll be ready to be eaten just a couple of weeks after sowing.

Are they easy to grow? Absolutely. You can grow microgreens almost anywhere—on a windowsill, countertop or container. All they need is a few inches of clean soil, four to six hours of sunlight and a daily misting with a spray bottle to keep them happy.

What should I plant? Any seed can be grown as a microgreen, but if you're just getting started, give arugula, beet, carrot, cilantro, cress, kale, peas, spinach or radish a try. Some packaged seed mixes contain a blend of popular varieties that will sprout at the same time.

How do you serve them? Eat microgreens raw and within a few days of harvesting. After snipping, gently rinse and pat them dry. Top soups and salads, fill sandwiches, or use microgreens to garnish appetizers or main dishes.

Indoor Planting in 5 Easy Steps

Want to grow microgreens at home? The process is simple!

1. Pick a spot that gets four to six hours of sunlight a day. The sill of a south-facing window is best.

2. Select a planting vessel (such as a shallow plastic tray, disposable pie plate or to-go container) and poke small holes in the bottom for adequate drainage.

3. Fill your container with 2 inches of clean potting medium and smooth until level. Scatter the seeds and lightly press them into the soil. Use a packaged mix for greens that will be ready to harvest at the same time, or grow a single crop. Spread a fine layer of soil on top.

4. Mist the soil daily with water from a spray bottle.

5. Snip the microgreens with scissors when they are $1\frac{1}{2}$ to 2 inches tall. Stagger planting to harvest weekly.

"I believe
the world is
incomprehensibly
beautiful—an
endless prospect of
magic and wonder."

—ANSEL ADAMS

Coral
hairstreak

UP CLOSE WITH LADYBUGS

Did you know that lady "bugs" are actually beetles? Get ready to learn even more about these beneficial backyard visitors.

Native ladybugs are harmless garden guests. It's their nonnative doppelgängers, Asian multicolored lady beetles, that can be bothersome as they enter and congregate in houses in search of warmth. You can identify the intruders by the dark M marking behind their heads.

There's a common belief that you can tell the beetle's age by how many spots it has, but this is a myth. While ladybugs can have as many as 16 spots, one of the most common varieties is the seven-spotted lady beetle, and some have no spots at all.

Ladybugs go by a few different names, including ladybirds, ladybugs, lady beetles and lady cows.

Ladybugs can eat up to 50 aphids a day. They also snack on mites, whiteflies, scale insects, mealybugs and thrips to protect your plants!

▼ ANTENNAE

Antennae, near the eyes, help poor-sighted ladybugs smell, taste and feel their way around.

▼ SHELL

Hard shells (elytra) cover and protect the wings.

▼ SPOTS

Black spots on the orange shell alert predators that this creature tastes bad.

▲ PRONOTUM

The pronotum is a platelike structure that protects the ladybug's head. It has two white dashes on top.

▲ LEGS

Short legs secrete poisonous gel if the bug is caught by a predator. The feet of the ladybug also help it smell.

DON'T SQUASH THAT BUG!

These oft-maligned garden visitors get a bad rap, but don't be too quick to shoo them away.

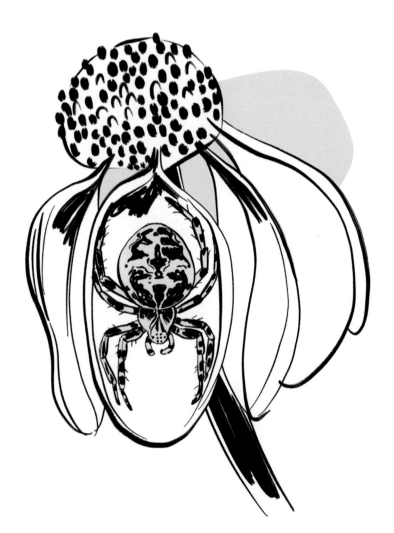

Caterpillars. Butterflies and moths are important pollinators, and their caterpillars attract birds to your yard. More than 95% of backyard birds rely on caterpillars as a primary food source for their young.

◄ SPIDERS

These arachnids are some of the most helpful garden invertebrates. All spiders feed on insects, whether they hunt using woven webs, by ambush or by stalking.

Bees, wasps and ants. All bee species are important pollinators and are largely responsible for the seeds, fruits and other plants that feed both people and wildlife. Wasps and ants are avid predators that can pick your garden clean of pests.

Predatory beetles and bugs. Mini predators such as tiger, soldier and ladybird beetles, along with assassin and pirate bugs, dine on their pesky plant-eating kin and protect your garden.

Dragonflies and damselflies. These aerial acrobats are a double threat. Adults feed on insects, including mosquitoes, biting flies and gnats, and their aquatic larvae devour the larvae of the same pests.

3 Visitors You Don't Want

These backyard guests tend to overstay their welcome. Show them the door!

MOSQUITOES

Mosquitoes cause itchy welts when they bite and also spread diseases. To keep them away, eliminate stagnant water in your yard (where mosquitoes breed) and wear insect repellent.

FIRE ANTS

These exotic ants were introduced to Alabama almost a century ago. They have an extremely painful sting and are displacing many native ant species. Avoid their large mounds, or call a professional exterminator.

TICKS

These parasitic arachnids spread diseases and can be particularly problematic in areas with large deer populations. Avoid tall grass, where ticks lie in wait. Mow pathways in your garden, wear long pants, and check yourself and pets after outdoor time.

MAKE ROOM FOR BIRDS

With a little planning, even the smallest outdoor space can be a haven for feathered friends.

◀ FOCUS ON THE BASICS

Birds are easy to please. If you give them food, water and shelter, they will visit backyards of any size—or even balconies, porches and patios.

Embrace the urban jungle. Urban areas can be as bird-friendly as large suburban backyards. After all, most large cities are built on rivers or lakes, which also happen to be migration pathways. All you have to do is entice the birds with some familiar scenery.

Plant with purpose. To maximize your space, choose plants that offer birds more than one resource, such as food, a place to build a nest and shelter from predators. Native berry-producing trees and shrubs are a triple-threat.

Think vertically. When ground space is limited, attract pollinators with cardinal vines and climbing nasturtiums; plant a dwarf tree; or consider window boxes, hanging planters or even tabletop pots.

No Yard?
No Problem!

The right supplies can help you enjoy birding even without a green space.

WINDOW FEEDERS
Suction cup feeders attach to your window and give you a close-up look at visiting birds. You'll have the best seat in the house!

HANGING BASKETS
Try displaying some hummingbird-friendly flowers in a basket on a balcony or patio. You might also attract butterflies and maybe even a sphinx moth.

BINOCULARS
If you live in a high-rise, look up: Peregrine falcons and red-tailed hawks patrol the skies in many urban areas. And look around for migrating birds in nearby treetops, as well as flocks of ducks, geese and gulls in flight.

Select super seeds. Black oil sunflower seed is the go-to meal for virtually all birds. It's an ideal option if you have space for only one feeder, or you can even sprinkle the seeds on the ground. Because the seeds are more fragile than striped sunflower, many birds can easily crack them open.

Provide a water source. Water can be even more effective than food in luring birds close. There are countless compact birdbath styles available, or you can make your own from just about anything. Moving water features will attract even more birds.

A Pal on the Patio

A lone scrub-jay showed up on my apartment patio a while back, so I started putting out unshelled, salt-free peanuts. We soon developed a ritual where I put out peanuts and it would fly in close to get them. When fall turned to winter, I didn't see my friend for a while, but it eventually returned for peanuts. Watching this jay and all the other birds that show up on my little patio has made me realize how very smart birds are.

—*Jeanne Martin*
Rifle, Colorado

PINT-SIZE OASIS

Create a miniature aquatic wonderland with a do-it-yourself pond. No fancy pumps or digging required!

Step 1. Choose your pond container. Ceramic, concrete, terra cotta, metal, plastic and porcelain are all great options, but don't use wood unless you line it with black plastic.

Step 2. Pick a spot. The pot will get heavy, so be sure to place it where you want to display it before filling it with water.

HEIDI HESS

Step 3. Add plants to the black plastic pots. If you're using heavy garden soil (high in clay content), cover the soil with an inch or two of pea gravel to keep it from floating. If you're using aquatic plant soil, bury a fertilizer tab with each plant so you won't have to fertilize.

Step 4. Place your potted plants at the appropriate depths in your empty pond container (you can use broken pieces of brick or upside-down terra cotta pots to help with this). Plant from deep to shallow and large to small.

Step 5. Add water to the potted plants themselves, then fill the container. Add your floater plants and the Mosquito Dunks doughnut. You're done!

The Supplies

Here's what you'll need:

- Watertight container
- Water plants
- Black plastic pots
- Garden soil (heavy clay) or aquatic plant soil
- Pea gravel (if using garden soil)
- Mosquito Dunks doughnut

The Plants

Look for three types of aquatic plants for your water garden:

EMERGENTS
Emergents are potted and have great foliage. Try umbrella palm and dwarf cattails.

SUBMERGED
Submerged plants live under the water and add oxygen. Try anacharis.

FLOATERS
True to their name, floaters float on the water's surface. Try water hyacinth and parrot's feathers.

TINY BUT MIGHTY

Anna's hummingbirds are a West Coast favorite. What makes them stand out from the crowd?

Anna's are more cold-hardy than other hummingbirds. They can be seen year-round along the Pacific Coast, as far north as Alaska. Their high-protein diet, which includes spiders, midges and leaf hoppers, might help them tolerate these colder conditions.

▶ **WEARING THE CROWN**
Anna's are the only North American hummingbirds that sport a full reddish crown. Males also display a brilliant magenta throat, called a gorget. Females have specks of pink-red on their throats, often forming a small gorget that is unusual for female hummingbirds.

Males put on a showy aerial mating display that starts with hovering in front of a female. They rise above the treetops (up to 130 feet), then dive downward, pulling up with a loud screech made by their tail feathers.

More vocal than most species of hummingbirds, male Anna's sing a buzzy, scratchy series of notes to attract a mate. Be advised—the song is hardly melodic to human ears!

BOB KOTHENBEUTEL

Male Anna's
hummingbird

Great
horned
owlets

WHAT'S THE WORD, BABY BIRD?

It's a big world out there—learn how baby birds hatch and grow before gaining their independence and taking flight.

◄ WHAT'S THE CORRECT TERM FOR BABY BIRDS?

While it's fine to call them babies or chicks, to be more specific, a young bird that has just hatched out of the egg is a hatchling, one that's still in the nest is a nestling and one that's left the nest is a fledgling.

How long does it take for birds to hatch? Many small songbirds need only 11 to 14 days of incubation. Some larger birds, such as hawks or geese, take about a month to hatch. And huge seabirds, such as albatrosses, need up to 80 days!

When do baby birds hatch? In North America, most birds nest in late spring and summer. Some birds, such as great horned owls, can hatch as early as January in certain areas, but American goldfinches may hatch as late as September.

What are the two types of baby birds?

Altricial young, which include those of most songbirds, hatch naked and with their eyes closed. Scrawny and pink, they can barely raise their heads at first. Precocial young, such as those of ducks and chickens, hatch covered with down. As soon as they dry off, they are alert and able to get up and walk.

What do baby birds eat?

Some species' chicks hatch with the instinct to find their own food. But birds that hatch naked sit in the nest and wait to be fed. Most songbird nestlings eat mainly protein-rich insects. Cedar waxwings bring insects to their young for the first two days but then start bringing a variety of fruits. American goldfinch babies get a diet of mashed-up seeds.

When do young birds leave the nest?

Downy baby ducks may follow their parents out of the nest within a few hours after hatching. Small songbirds, which develop rapidly thanks to their parents constantly bringing them food, may leave the nest 8 to 12 days after hatching. And very big birds, such as the California condor, may stay in the nest for six months.

How do young birds learn to fly?

Many songbird fledglings can barely fly but manage well enough to avoid predators and find food. On the other hand, the young of swallows, which feed on flying insects, wait until their wings are fully developed before they take off. Flight is so critical to their lifestyle that the young stay close to their parents and may learn to fly partly from watching them.

Female Anna's hummingbird and nestlings

Can young birds care for themselves after they leave the nest? Fledglings have it tough: They need to find enough food and learn to recognize predators and other dangers. It takes trial and error, but if they can survive for a few weeks, they have a good chance of living a normal life span.

How can I help baby birds? Providing native plants, keeping cats indoors and avoiding pesticides can support young birds in your area. In return, you'll get the joy of watching them grow up and explore their world.

RAISING ROBINS

Time flies! Let's follow a robin's typical journey from egg to independence.

Day 1. The female robin begins to build a cup-shaped nest out of twigs and grass with a mud base. Her mate brings her bits of material as she constructs the nest.

Day 8. The female lays her first egg. Robins tend to lay clutches of three or four solid blue eggs and can raise three or more broods per year.

Day 9. The female lays her second egg.

Day 10. The female lays her third egg. She may begin incubating.

Day 11. The female lays her fourth egg and commits to incubating.

Day 22. The first egg begins to hatch.

Day 24. The last egg finishes hatching. The female broods the hatchlings to keep them warm.

▲ DAYS 25–36

Both parents bring food for the young robins, eventually delivering 100 to 150 meals a day to the nest. Each nestling may eat its weight in insects, worms and berries per day.

Day 37. All the young begin to leave the nest. The adults continue to feed the fledglings as they explore the surrounding areas.

▼ DAYS 58-65

The young robins become independent. During their first summer, they sport dark-spotted breasts, along with buff speckling across their backs.

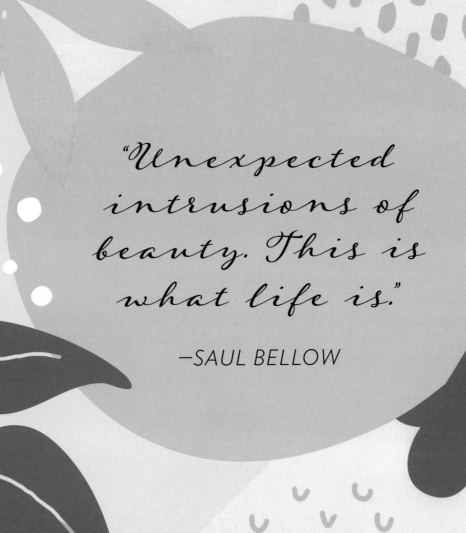

"Unexpected intrusions of beauty. This is what life is."

—SAUL BELLOW

Rufous
hummingbird
perched on
hawk's beard

The Backyard Pantry

HARVEST TIME IS HERE AT LAST, AND THE GARDEN IS OVERFLOWING WITH EDIBLE ABUNDANCE. ARE YOU READY TO DIG IN?

Growing your own food is a labor of love. Tending and toiling in the garden for months is no small feat, but a perfectly ripe tomato, a bunch of fragrant herbs or a pool of amber honey can make the efforts feel instantly worthwhile. And don't forget the way a bumper crop of zucchini can make you the star of the neighborhood! Take a tour of what's in stock—from the root cellar to the chicken coop—and prepare your table for a feast.

TIPS FOR A STELLAR ROOT CELLAR

A cool basement and traditional techniques can keep your garden crops fresh through the winter. All you need to succeed is a little know-how.

Keep it moist. Dry air draws moisture away from produce, leading to shriveled crops all too quickly. To prevent this, keep the humidity at around 90%. Yes, that's high, but dirt floors naturally hold moisture, and you can place damp towels over the tops of produce bins to maintain humidity.

Keep it cool. Before modern refrigeration, this was how people kept much of their produce from decomposing. Ideally, a root cellar will hold produce at a temperature between 32 and 40 degrees.

Keep it dark. Produce stores much better out of direct sunlight, which will break it down quickly. Sunlight also encourages the roots to send up shoots, rendering the food inedible. If possible, root cellars should be windowless; if you have windows, be sure they are sealed and well covered.

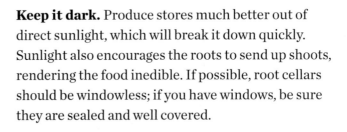

▲ CHOOSE THE RIGHT CROPS

Certain crops lend themselves better to winter storage and eating than others. Potatoes, onions, shallots, beets, squash, carrots, cabbages and turnips top the list.

Give fruit a chance. Most fruits aren't suited to cold storage, but apples and pears will fare well in a root cellar. Space them out on wooden shelves with their stems up, or wrap them individually with tissue paper and store them in wooden boxes.

Store smart. If you're storing a few varieties of the same vegetable or fruit, put the longest-lasting variety at the bottom of the bin for the best results. Keep apples and pears away from other produce in your cellar; they give off ethylene, which hastens ripening.

THE DIRT ON CARROTS

These root cellar superstars bring a lot more than crunch to the table.

More than 85% of U.S. carrots are grown in California. Michigan and Texas are also among the top carrot-growing states.

Carrots are an incredible source of beta carotene, vitamin C and potassium, but they're especially high in vitamin A. Half a cup of carrots contains about 204% of your recommended daily value.

The average person eats more than 10,000 carrots in their lifetime. On a yearly basis, one person will munch on 8.3 pounds of fresh carrots and consume 1.4 pounds of the veggie from the freezer.

Orange wasn't always the most prevalent color of carrot. Prior to the 1600s, purple and yellow were most common.

"White" carrots are actually available in five colors: orange, red, yellow, white and purple.

The Root of the Problem

Horticulture expert Melinda Myers digs deep to answer tricky questions about root vegetables.

Q I tried my luck at growing radishes in a pot. They sprouted beautifully and had five leaves, but then nothing happened. What's going on?
—*Elizabeth Barnhart*
Bakersfield, California

MELINDA: All leaves and no roots is a common complaint from gardeners who grow radishes. When it comes to achieving full-sized roots, well-draining soil, thinning and proper fertilization are key. Avoid high-nitrogen fertilizers, which encourage top growth and discourage root development. Once two true leaves have developed, thin the seedlings to about 1 inch apart. This creates room for the roots to reach full size. Use the removed leaves as greens for salads, sandwiches and snacks. If you're still having trouble, test the soil to see if it needs phosphorus, which encourages root growth.

Q Can you share some information about growing the vegetable salsify?
—*Carol Groves*
Roanoke, Virginia

MELINDA: Salsify needs deep loose soil to form its long and slender roots. Many gardeners have greater success growing it in raised beds, where they can create the best soil conditions. Salsify needs 120 to 150 days to reach mature size, so plant the seeds as soon as the soil can be worked. Harvest the roots after a light frost or when they are 1 to 1½ inches in diameter. Another option is to leave them in the garden over winter. Just mulch the soil lightly and harvest before spring. This root vegetable has no serious pests, but heavy and poorly draining soils may prevent the roots from reaching full size.

Scarlet
runner
beans

SEED STORAGE SECRETS

Follow these simple steps to store and replant seeds from your tastiest produce.

◀ PICK THE BEST SEEDS

Save the seeds from your best-tasting crops. Pepper, tomato and cucumber seeds are all best when harvested from vine-ripened and mature produce, but seeds from peas and beans are best picked after they've dried on the plants.

Wash carefully. Remove the seeds from your produce and strip away any excess flesh, then rinse the seeds in a colander under cold water. Be gentle—don't scratch them! Scatter the seeds on a paper towel and let them dry fully.

Store wisely. Place the dried seeds in a labeled paper envelope and keep them somewhere cool, dark and dry until planting season.

Test them out. A few weeks before planting, take out a dozen or so seeds, wrap them in a wet paper towel and keep them in a plastic bag in a warm spot. The proportion of seeds that germinate in a week or two will tell you how many of your seeds will likely sprout in soil.

Beware of biennials and hybrids. Biennial crops like carrots and beets take two years to produce seeds. Hybrids tend to cross-pollinate and won't breed true to type.

PRESERVE YOUR HERBS

Stretch your garden's bounty by stocking your pantry with home-dried herbs.

Timing your harvest. In most cases, leaves provide the herbs' flavors and should be picked before the flowers develop. Harvest leaves on warm, dry days, early in the morning after the dew has evaporated. Discard any damaged or diseased leaves before drying.

Rack drying. Spacing out sprigs or leaves on a tray hastens drying for large-leaved herbs like bay. Place the tray in an airing cupboard, warming drawer, or warm and airy spot out of direct sunlight. Turn the herbs frequently to ensure even drying, which should take two or three days.

Oven drying. The leaves of herbs such as rosemary, mint, sage, parsley and thyme, stripped from their stalks, are ideal for oven drying. Space out leaves on a muslin-covered tray, then place the tray in an oven set to the lowest temperature. Leave the door ajar and flip the leaves after 30 minutes; they will be quite dry after an hour.

Air-drying. Tie sprigs or branches of tarragon, mint, lavender, thyme or rosemary into small bunches to allow adequate aeration. Hang the bunches with the leaves downward, wrapped loosely in muslin or thin paper bags (plastic bags can promote mold development). On average, allow 7 to 10 days of drying time; when crushed, the leaves should sound like crisp cornflakes.

Storing your herbs. Crumble the dried herbs, and discard the hard leafstalks and midribs. Store in small airtight containers, preferably made of pottery or opaque glass. If you're using a glass jar, store it in a dark place so the herbs don't lose their color.

Using your herbs. Drying concentrates the flavors of herbs, so you don't need to use as much in recipes. If a recipe calls for a specific measurement of fresh herbs, use one-third that amount of dried herbs instead.

RULES OF THE ROOST

Forget the old adage about the chicken or the egg—it's a well-designed coop that comes first.

▶ VENTILATE WISELY

Position vents up high to prevent drafts and under overhangs to keep out snow and rain. Covering vents in wire keeps out predators and pests.

Safety. Building a coop like a fort may seem to be overkill, but it's a worthwhile precaution. Hardware cloth is stronger than so-called chicken wire and provides better protection for the birds. Bury it around the entire perimeter to thwart digging animals.

▶ PROTECT THE HENS

Raccoons, weasels and other critters can fit through surprisingly tight openings. Any open spaces should be covered!

Ventilation. Chickens need fresh air year-round. The birds' breath and droppings generate humidity, and damp litter can increase a flock's risk of infections and worsen their footpad condition and respiratory health. A good coop needs an adequate inlet and outlet for proper airflow.

Comfort. Hens need a cozy place with plenty of bedding (such as straw or sawdust) to lay their eggs. Nesting boxes should be kept out of the way to prevent disturbances. Putting a few plastic eggs in the box can also encourage laying. Nesting boxes with slanted roofs keep chickens from roosting on top.

Cleanliness. Protecting chickens from disease is far easier than treating it. Clothing that's been around other chickens should be cleaned and disinfected, and every year the entire coop should be washed, dried and then sprayed with a diluted disinfectant (like bleach) in a garden sprayer.

◄ GATHER THE EGGS
Gathering eggs is easier if nesting boxes are accessible from the outside. A lock protects the eggs.

◄ SUPPLEMENT THE FEED
Include a calcium source (such as oyster shell or limestone) in the feed to help laying hens build eggshell.

CHICKEN PICKS

Many chicken breeds make good backyard egg-layers. These five breeds each bring something different to the table.

◀ COCHIN

Weight: 8.5 lbs. **Eggs:** Large
Temperament: Huggable

Big, plush Cochins almost resemble teddy bears. Their thick feathers come in many colors, including black, buff, blue, white, partridge and barred. Cochins are friendly and easily tamed, and they often act broody, protecting their eggs. These hens are big enough to hatch duck or turkey eggs.

▶ SILKIE

Weight: 2 lbs. **Eggs:** Medium
Temperament: Docile

Known for downy soft feathers, black eyes and slate blue skin, this bantam breed makes a great pet. The plumage, which comes bearded or nonbearded in black, blue, partridge, buff, white or gray, looks and feels like silky, fluffy fur. The hens are small, so they're easy to pick up. You'll want to pet them often.

▲ AMERAUCANA

Weight: 5.5 lbs. **Eggs:** Large
Temperament: Gentle
Folks love these hens for their colored eggs. Ameraucanas were developed as a cold-hardy breed, and their fluffy faces are bearded and muffed, adding to their beauty. Pretty plumage varieties include black, blue, silver, wheaten, white and lavender.

▼ POLISH

Weight: 4.5 lbs. **Eggs:** Medium
Temperament: Calm
This flashy breed likely originated in Spain, not Poland, but the feathered caps worn by Polish soldiers may have inspired the name—the small birds have crests on their heads. They are usually placid, but having obscured vision may make them nervous. Try not to surprise or startle them.

◄ WYANDOTTE

Weight: 6.5 lbs. **Eggs:** Large
Temperament: Friendly
Originally known as American Sebrights, these birds are popular for their eye-catching patterns and colors, such as partridge, Columbian, golden laced, blue, and silver-penciled. The hens are good mothers and prolific egg-layers, making them a valuable addition to any family's flock.

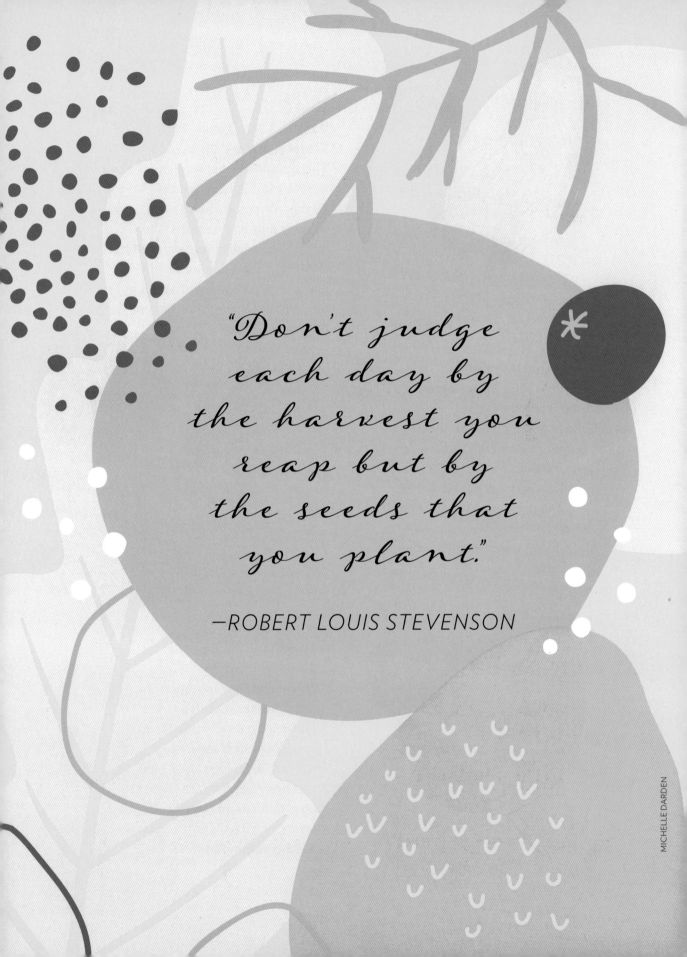

"Don't judge each day by the harvest you reap but by the seeds that you plant."

—ROBERT LOUIS STEVENSON

MICHELLE DARDEN

COMMON TOMATO MISTAKES

Vine-ripe tomatoes are one of summer's great joys. Avoid these missteps and you'll be on your way to harvesting a bumper crop.

◀ PASSING ON PRUNING

Tomato plants tend to get leggy—and that's fine! Just remember to prune them strategically. Early in the season, trim away small stems (or "suckers") along the base and stem of the plant. This will focus the plant's energy on creating a strong main stem. About a month before the end of the growing season, snip off the very top of the tomato plant. This will encourage the plant to ripen the last fruits instead of growing taller.

Picking the same spot every year.
Changing location can reduce the risk of insects and disease. Plus, all plants draw nutrients from the soil, and tomatoes in particular soak up a lot. If space allows, switch up where you grow your plants. If not, be sure to replenish the soil with compost and fertilizer.

Skipping companion plants.
While companion plants aren't necessary, certain plants improve the soil and others shelter helpful insects that eat garden pests.

Planting the wrong type.
Determinate tomatoes, which grow
to a particular height and produce
all their fruit in a short time span,
work well for folks who want to
harvest many tomatoes at once (say,
for canning). Indeterminate plants,
which continue to produce fruit
until frost hits or you pinch off the
growing tips, are better if you want
access to fresh tomatoes throughout
the summer. Choose wisely!

Using small pots. When it comes
to planting tomatoes in containers,
bigger is better. They need plenty of
nutrient-rich soil and enough room
to put down roots. Also, larger pots
hold moisture longer than small
ones, so you won't have to water
as frequently.

▼ THINKING ALL HEIRLOOM TOMATOES ARE THE SAME

The word *heirloom* is a catchall
term for heritage varieties that
haven't changed over time. They
offer different shapes, colors and
flavors, so find out what makes a
particular heirloom variety special
before settling on a pick.

Growing too close together. Crowding your plants limits the sun and airflow the leaves get. If plants don't get all the fresh air and sunlight they need, they'll yield less fruit or possibly develop diseases. Give tomato plants ample room to grow—about 3 feet between each plant is best, depending on the variety.

Placing in the shade. Tomato plants require full sun—a shady spot just won't work. If sun is at a premium in your yard, give your tomatoes the best spot. Other veggies (such as beets, carrots and greens) can handle a bit of shade.

Staking after they're unruly. Tomatoes need the support of stakes or cages, and the best time to give that support is before they really need it. Plus, smaller plants are easier to adjust.

Planting too early. Don't rush to plant tomatoes the second the snow melts. Instead, wait until freezing temperatures are long past (the plants won't survive a frost without cover). Read the instructions on seed packets and plant tags to know when to start the growing season.

Fertilizing at the wrong time. Avoid high-nitrogen fast-release fertilizers when tomatoes are in their prime, as those fertilizers promote leaf and stem growth, not flower and fruit production. For months of benefits, try a slow-release fertilizer at planting. And always follow the instructions on the label!

BACKYARD PRODUCE MYTHS

Bad advice abounds when it comes to planting and harvesting produce in a backyard garden. We're here to sort fact from fiction.

MYTH:

Veggies don't need full sun.

REALITY:

Vegetables always produce best in full sun. Tomatoes, peppers and other plants that produce edible flowers and fruits need the most sunlight—eight hours or more. Root crops, such as beets and radishes, can produce with four to six hours of full sun.

MYTH:

If you plant cucumbers next to pumpkins, they cross-pollinate and ruin the harvest.

REALITY:

When bees carry pollen from one plant to another, cross-pollination can occur, but it affects the seeds, not the fruit you eat. If you plant the seeds in next year's garden, however, you might be in for a surprise.

MYTH:

Adding sugar to the soil will make tomatoes sweeter.

REALITY:

Sugar can actually stunt the growth of plants. If you want sweeter tomatoes, look for varieties intentionally bred to be sweeter.

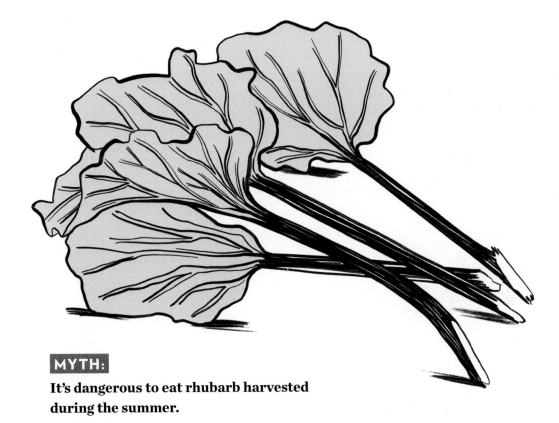

MYTH:

It's dangerous to eat rhubarb harvested during the summer.

REALITY:

You can eat rhubarb stalks from spring through fall, but the flavor is best when they are harvested in the first 8 to 10 weeks of the season. Rhubarb leaves do contain oxalic acid, which can be toxic in high amounts, so don't eat those.

MYTH:

To ripen green tomatoes, set them on a sunny windowsill.

REALITY:

Sunlight isn't needed. For slow ripening, wrap tomatoes in newspaper to contain the ethylene gas that hastens ripening and put them in a cool basement. For faster results, store ripe and unripe fruits together.

MYTH:

The reason pepper plants aren't setting fruit is because the soil is too rich.

REALITY:

Overly rich soil will favor foliage over flowers, but it won't stop pepper plants from bearing fruit altogether. The weather is a more likely culprit. Flowers can drop off below 55 degrees or above 85 degrees, or in a hot, drying wind.

Field Notes

A Birdy Buffet

This yellow-rumped warbler came to eat a ripening persimmon fruit last October. The bird has been an autumn visitor to our Southern California yard for the last several years. I've also spotted it eating suet in the winter.

—James Tucker
Ventura, California

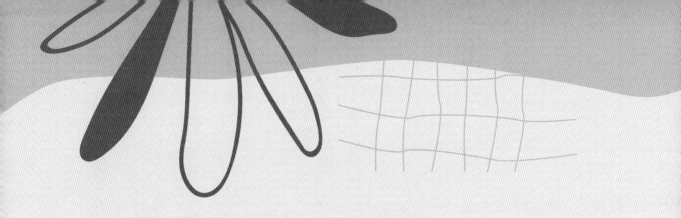

Reader Secrets:
Use Up Extra Veggies

Readers share their creative tips for making the most out of an abundance of produce.

Roy, my husband, loads up extra produce in his tractor and drives around the neighborhood to give it away. Who needs an ice cream man when you have a fresh veggie man?
—*Shawnda Hurley*
Kelso, Washington

My husband and I live in a senior community where we have a raised-bed garden. We put our extra veggies in a decorative box for residents who are unable to grow their own.
—*Carol Brisky*
Canby, Oregon

We give leftover strawberries and corn to our goats and chickens.
—*Megan McCloud*
Woodbine, Maryland

My home-based business lets me share with clients. They swap their harvest with me too!
—*Lorraine Schmit*
Mass City, Michigan

When I'm lucky enough to have extra tomatoes, I roast them with garlic and olive oil and freeze them in 2-cup portions. It's the perfect base for a pasta sauce.
—*Kathy Eppers*
Aledo, Texas

I leave out leftover sliced carrots for the chipmunks, deer and rabbits in my backyard.
—*Mike Froio*
Rome, New York

ADVENTURES IN BEEKEEPING

Join horticulture expert Melinda Myers on a journey from hive novice to queen bee.

"I've always wanted to raise bees." That offhand comment was all it took for my friend Pete to give me a beekeeping gift for Mother's Day, complete with a bee box and a how-to book. But Pete's thoughtful present arrived a little late to order bees, so it sat in my garage for over a year. When spring arrived, my daughter told a beekeeper friend about my failure to launch, and the next thing I knew, veteran beekeepers Cesar Cerna and Carol Kremer were buzzing around my yard, ready to help me get my hive off the ground.

The first thing I needed was a complete bee box. I had a 10-frame super (the structure that holds the bees), but I lacked inner and outer covers, a bottom and a stand. I also didn't have a protective veil or gloves. Or bees. But Cesar and Carol patiently helped me order everything I needed.

One thing I did have was a nice sunny spot for the hive among the fruit trees and flowers in my garden. Sheltered inside a fenced area, it'd also be safe from strong winds and critters.

I started my hive with a nucleus colony, which includes a fertilized queen, larvae, combs and honey. We set the five-frame nucleus colony inside the 10-frame super, added the lid, set out some sugar water and let the bees settle into their new home.

After a week or two, Cesar and Carol came back to help me check on the queen. We needed to make sure she hadn't packed her bags instead of producing offspring. Luckily, we soon spotted white ricelike eggs and healthy, pearly white larvae and pupae in capped cells. Things were going so well that I had to expand their home with another super. I also started to see many bees visiting my flowerbeds.

Two months in, it was time to add a half-super for the bees to store honey. Although the colony had been coming along nicely, the wooden stand was not holding up to outdoor conditions as well as I'd hoped, so Pete and I put together a new one made of tough cement blocks.

We then needed to figure out how to transfer the heavy bee- and honey-filled hive to its new stand. We definitely didn't want to agitate the bees. But Cesar and Carol came to the rescue once again. We smoked the hive to keep the bees calm during the move. The smoke hinders their sense of smell, which bees use to communicate. Normally, if there's a hive intruder, bees release an alarm pheromone to ready a group attack. If they can't smell the pheromone, they stay calm.

Home Sweet Home

Take a tour of a honeybee hive.

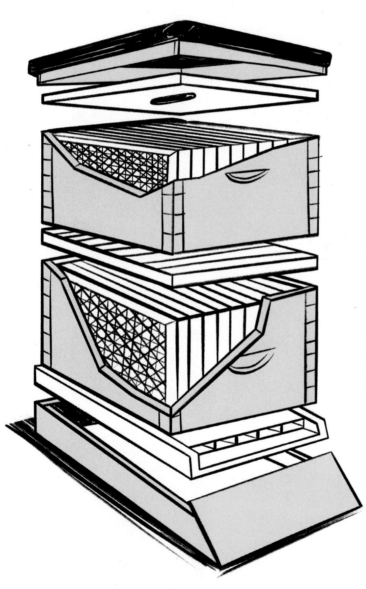

◄ **OUTER COVER**
Sits on top of the hive to protect bees from harsh weather.

◄ **INNER COVER**
Goes over the uppermost super.

◄ **HONEY SUPER**
Contains frames for honey storage.

◄ **QUEEN EXCLUDER**
Prevents the queen from laying eggs in the honey super.

◄ **DEEP SUPER**
Contains frames to house bees.

◄ **BOTTOM BOARD**
Is the floor of the hive.

◄ **STAND**
Elevates the hive to reduce any damage to the bottom board from dampness.

Excited to share the hive progress with Pete, once the bees were soothed, Cesar handed Pete a bee-filled frame. Pete hadn't expected to be so involved! Then it was time to hold the bee-filled super, which probably weighed over 50 pounds. Pete later told me that he was so focused on the risk of an angry bee flying up his shorts that he didn't even notice how heavy the super was.

The good news is that none of us, including the bees, were harmed during the move. Once everyone was settled in again, the super filled up fast, and I added a second one a month later. I left the honey for the bees this first year so they'd have plenty of food to get them through the winter. Straw bales now surround the hive to keep the bees warm throughout the winter; they'll huddle inside to live off their honey stores until next spring, when the flowers will bloom and my honeybees will return to my backyard garden.

A Beekeeper's Toolkit

Get the right supplies for success!

- **Bee brush:** Helps gently move bees out of the way during hive inspections.
- **Hive tool:** A mini crowbar for lifting off the sealed top and frames for inspections.
- **Jacket with veil and gloves:** Protective clothing that increases your comfort level when working with bees.
- **Smoker:** Calms bees, reducing the beekeeper's risk of being stung.
- **Super:** A box with 8 to 10 frames in which bees build honeycombs.

HONEYBEES BY THE NUMBERS

Learn the sweet truth about these industrious honey producers.

20

There are over 20 subspecies of western honeybee, none of which are native to North America. They spread here after being brought from Europe, the Middle East and Africa.

2,000

Queen bees are the only females that reproduce. The pheromones the queen releases prevent worker bees from making eggs, so she remains the mother and star of the hive. On any given day, a queen bee is able to lay up to 2,000 eggs.

7

The lifespan of a bee depends on where it falls within the colony. Queens live up to seven years; workers born in spring or early summer live only five to six weeks.

1/12

According to the American Beekeeping Federation, the average honeybee will produce only 1/12 teaspoon of honey over the course of its life.

4

Honeybees have four wings, which they use to fly up to 20 mph. Their speed and stamina allow them to forage for pollen up to 2 miles away from the hive.

230

As honeybees fly, a buzzing sound follows them through the air. The sound is their wings flapping 230 times per second.

3,000

Honey keeps indefinitely, thanks in part to its high sugar content, low water content and high acidity. Archaeologists have found 3,000-year-old pots of honey, still unspoiled, in Egyptian tombs.

55,000

Collectively, honeybees need to fly more than 55,000 miles (more than twice the earth's circumference!) and visit two million flowers to produce 1 pound of honey.

80

Honeybees pollinate 80% of all U.S. vegetable and seed crops.

Dandelion
potato salad,
dandelion salad,
dandelion soup

DELICIOUS DANDELIONS

Learn more about these bright—and edible—harbingers of spring.

◀ ALL YOU CAN EAT

Every part of this versatile plant is edible. You can eat the roots raw, cook them like a vegetable, or roast and grind them into a caffeine-free coffee substitute. The flowers can be turned into dandelion wine or jellies, added to salads, or dipped in batter and fried as fritters. The leaves can be eaten raw, steamed, boiled, sauteed or stir-fried; add them to omelets, salads, soups, sandwiches and even smoothies.

Dandelions are part of the daisy family. They can reach heights up to 24 inches, and their roots go as deep as 10 to 15 feet. And though you may think of each sunny yellow burst as one flower, a dandelion head actually consists of up to 300 individual ray flowers.

There's evidence that dandelion seeds, native to Europe and Asia, came to North America on the Mayflower. Colonists planted the herb around their homesteads to use for food and as dyes for fiber (yellow from the flower, magenta from the roots).

For centuries, dandelions have been used as a cure-all for everything from fever and lethargy to toothaches and warts. Modern studies confirm that dandelions are a good source of vitamins A and C, thiamin, riboflavin and folate, plus minerals such as iron, potassium and zinc.

▲ WHAT'S IN A NAME?

Dandelions' Latin name, *Taraxacum officinale*, means "the official remedy for disorders," hearkening back to their medicinal uses. The common name, however, comes from the French *dent-de-lion*, or "lion's tooth," because of their serrated leaves.

The best time to harvest wild dandelion greens is in early spring, before flowers appear, when they're most tender and least bitter. When well prepared, the flavor is refreshing and tangy, with a bit of a bite. More pungent mature greens can be blanched to remove bitterness.

Look for dandelions in rich, deep soil where the ground is porous and well-watered, and where grass grows tall and free. Avoid areas sprayed with herbicides, near roadsides or railroad tracks. Always rinse flowers, stems and leaves well before using. Thoroughly clean roots to remove dirt and debris.

Share with Backyard Visitors

Dandelions aren't just good for your dinner plate—they'll be visited and appreciated by local wildlife too.

If you've got more dandelions in your yard than you can use in your kitchen, let the rest grow! Dandelion seeds ripen just in time to nourish goldfinches and indigo buntings during their spring migrations. Goldfinches and hummingbirds will also use fluffy dandelion fibers to line their nests. And letting your dandelions flower will attract welcome pollinators such as bees and butterflies.

FROM GARDEN TO GLASS

These plants add a jolt of flavor to cocktails, teas and other beverages.

Chocolate Mint
Mentha x *piperita f. citrata*, **Zones 5 to 9.** The leaves of this fast-growing plant smell like chocolate but have a minty orange taste. Steep them in hot water to make chocolate-mint tea, or make a simple syrup for mojitos and gin sodas.

Common Juniper
Juniperus communis, **Zones 2 to 7.** This conifer's berries (actually tiny blue cones) are used to flavor gin and some beers. Add them to gin fizzes, gin and tonic cocktails, champagne, tea or lemonade. Note: Some junipers are poisonous, so research your plant before picking!

Parisian Gherkin F1 Cucumbers
Cucumi sativus, **Annual.** These mini black-spined gherkin cucumbers are great fresh or pickled. Harvest the cukes regularly when they are 2 to 4 inches long. Use them in vodka martinis or cucumber Collins, or mix them with gin, lime and mint.

Mojito

Garden Party Tips

Enjoy your garden with friends by hosting an outdoor cocktail hour.

SWEETEN THE DEAL
Make your own infused simple syrup by simmering ½ cup herbs, flowers or fruits with 1 cup each sugar and water until the sugar dissolves. Strain, cool and refrigerate for up to two weeks.

GROW GREAT GARNISHES
You eat (and drink) with your eyes first. Float a marigold bloom on a blood orange martini, scatter lavender petals atop a blackberry agua fresca or dress up a glass of champagne with a pretty pansy.

SET THE SCENE
Plant a fountain, a few chairs and a bistro table near your garden. Your friends will happily sip their freshly picked beverages while drinking up the fresh air.

Roselle Hibiscus
Hibiscus sabdariffa, **Zones 8 to 11.** This bold plant features crimson stems, red-veined leaves and pink flowers. Its flowers and calyxes lend a tangy, cranberrylike taste to drinks. Add it to rose hip tea with dried orange peel or a squeeze of lime.

English Lavender
Lavandula angustifolia, **Zones 5 to 8.** Lavender's sweet floral notes pair well with berries, pears and citrus flavors when used sparingly in a simple syrup or as a fresh mix-in. Use it in lavender-sage slings, gin sours, hot or iced tea, lemonade or seltzer.

Siam Queen Thai Basil
Ocimum basilicum var. thyrsiflora, **Zones 10 to 11.** This plant's purple stems and flowers pack a punch with hints of licorice and lemon. Plant fresh batches each year for maximum flavor. Add the leaves to gimlets, martinis, daiquiris or lemonade. Its flowers make pretty garnishes too.

▲ ALPINE STRAWBERRY

Fragaria vesca, **Zones 5 to 9.** Also known as wild or woodland strawberry, this decorative perennial bears fruit throughout the growing season. The berries add interest to cordials or rosé and can be used to make strawberry-basil lemonade.

Lemon Verbena

Aloysia citriodora, **Zones 8 to 10 or Annual.** The citrusy spear-shaped leaves of this sun-loving perennial can be harvested by cutting the entire stem. Add them to gin and tonic or gimlet cocktails. The fresh or dried leaves and the blossoms all make great iced tea, too—try combining the verbena with mint and honey.

BEYOND BIRDSEED

Birds enjoy more than seed, suet and sugar water. Make your buffet the best on the block with a few new treats.

Fruit. Everything from brilliantly colored tanagers to butterflies will flock to fruit. Orioles love orange halves; when they've eaten the fruit, fill the empty peels with jelly. Also try putting out berries or raisins—you might just attract mockingbirds or robins.

Roasted seeds. To go beyond the usual sunflower and safflower varieties, try roasting pumpkin or squash seeds—Northern cardinals, sparrows and other seed specialists will especially enjoy the variety. Just be sure to serve them plain, not seasoned.

Baked eggshells. Eggshells provide calcium, which can be especially important for females during mating season. Be sure to wash and bake the shells to kill off any potential pathogens. Crush the shells and add them to seed, then just sprinkle them on the ground or offer them in a platform feeder.

Jelly. Grape jelly is becoming a go-to offering for orioles. Gray catbirds and red-bellied woodpeckers also can't seem to resist the sweet fruity stuff. Any shallow container will do the trick.

▼ MEALWORMS

Mealworms are like candy to a wide range of birds, including some species that don't usually come to traditional feeders, like bluebirds and robins. If you're offering live mealworms, the feeder should be at least a couple of inches deep to keep the worms from crawling out.

Peanut butter. Woodpeckers and blue jays relish peanut butter snacks. You can stuff it in the holes of a log feeder or even just smear it on tree bark.

Red-bellied woodpecker with mealworms

OFF THE MENU

Avoid these foods to keep your backyard birds healthy.

Bacon fat. This fat is very salty, has additives and spoils easily. To make suet, get high-quality fat straight from the butcher, before it gets processed.

Pet food. Dog and cat kibble lack nutrition for birds and may attract mice, rats or other backyard pests.

Red dye. There's no need to add any food coloring to your hummingbird sugar water. The dye is harmful and won't attract more birds.

Raw meat. It might seem like a good idea to set out raw meat as a winter treat, but it can go rancid and spoil—and attract unwanted guests.

Old birdseed. Serve fresh seed to ensure your backyard friends aren't exposed to moldy or rancid food.

Potato chips. While this popular snack is often a staple at outdoor gatherings, it doesn't provide proper nutrition. Keep these morsels for the people at your next picnic.

▲ BREAD
Many people like
to feed bread to
ducks and other
birds, but it fills
them up quickly,
causing them to
skip out on more
nutritious foods.

**Seeds and nuts sold
for people.** Sunflower
seeds and legumes
made for humans often
have large amounts
of salt. Birdseed is
produced specifically
for birds, leaving out
the extra sodium.

Honey. You'd
think birds could
use the calories
and sugar, but
contaminated
honey can grow
mold—and be
troublesome
and sticky.

"The sun, with all those planets revolving around it and dependent on it, can still ripen a bunch of grapes as if it had nothing else in the universe to do."

—GALILEO GALILEI

CHAPTER 4

The Wonder of Water

DIP YOUR TOE INTO A FASCINATING WATERY WORLD—AND LEARN HOW THIS VITAL RESOURCE HELPS NATURE THRIVE.

From the soothing patter of a summer rain to the bright splashing of a robin in a birdbath, water has a way of demanding our attention. But it's not just the gurgles, babbles, glugs and drips that keep us captivated—where there's water, plant and animal life abound. Journey with us through reeds and rain gardens alike as we dive into the myriad ways water ripples through the natural world.

Sora
rail

MARVELOUS MARSHES

Marshes are some of the most productive ecosystems in the world. Which birds call this habitat home?

◄ RAILS

These thin marsh dwellers can easily slip through dense vegetation, allowing them to feed and nest in the thickest cattail stands. They're secretive but quite vocal, often heard rather than seen.

Marsh wrens. Marsh wrens are small brown birds with cocked tails and chattering voices. The male stakes out a section of cattails, then builds several softball-sized nests and has them ready for the female's inspection when she arrives. She's choosy: She might accept one of the nests, build her own or move on to another male's territory.

▼ HERONS AND EGRETS

All sizes of herons and egrets frequent marshes to feed on the many species of fish, reptiles and amphibians that flourish there. Northern marshes are oft frequented by great blue herons, black-crowned night herons, and great and snowy egrets.

Waterfowl. North America is home to dozens of species of ducks, geese and swans, and almost all of them spend time in marshes. One species to watch for is the ruddy duck—a small, stocky, colorful bird that's easy to identify: Males are cinnamon red with a dark head and a bright blue bill.

Great blue heron

Gulls and terns.

Franklin's gulls and Forester's and black terns usually build their nests away from the shore on floating dead vegetation, keeping their eggs just slightly above the water. They eat aquatic insects, many of which are caught on the fly, and small fish and crustaceans.

Red-winged blackbirds.

You can't have a marsh without this bold bird. These jet-black beauties have scarlet wing patches. You can usually find them perched on a cattail head, with wings spread wide, singing *kon-kon-ka-ree*.

Harsh Marsh or Land of Plenty?

The same factors that keep many humans out draw abundant bird life to the marsh ecosystem.

To most people, a marsh isn't a very appealing place. Gooey mud borders water covered with thick algae. The smell is often pungent—and usually not very pleasant. Also, the vegetation is so dense that it's nearly impossible to force your way through.

Yet marshes have everything that birds need to prosper. Clouds of mosquitoes and other insects that bedevil humans provide a constant supply of protein to adult birds and growing chicks, and the thick vegetation gives both a secure nesting place and a refuge from predators. It's an avian paradise!

Shorebirds. Larger birds, such as the American avocet and white-faced ibis, and small species of sandpipers and plovers make their living on the muddy edges of marshes. The small species race along the shoreline to feed on tiny insects and crustaceans.

American bitterns. Technically in the heron family, bitterns don't act like most other herons. They are very secretive as they slip through the vegetation. If they think they've been detected, they freeze, standing up straight, their brown plumage blending in with dead cattails.

◄ COMMON YELLOWTHROATS

These tiny warblers sport a bright yellow throat, an olive gray body and a black bandit's mask around their eyes. When defending his territory, the male yellowthroat sits on a cattail or other high perch, singing *wichety, wichety, wichety.*

Raptors. Northern harriers (once called marsh hawks), bald eagles and great horned owls hunt in marshes for birds and other small animals.

FRANCIS C BERGQUIST

- Field Notes -

Among the Reeds

American bitterns are often difficult to see, but when these young ones galumphed around the marsh, it gave me a prime opportunity to capture them in their typical pose of "I am just a reed." Bitterns will shift back and forth in sync with the marsh grasses swaying in the breeze. It's a fascinating survival skill that makes them tricky to spot.

—*Douglas Beall*
Camp Sherman, Oregon

SWAMP THINGS

Banish thoughts of deep shadows, dark water and lurking creatures—from colorful warblers to elegant storks, unexpected avian beauty is all around you when you step into a swamp.

◀ WHITE IBISES

Contrary to their name, young white ibises are mostly brown, but adults are as white as cotton. Similar in size and color to snowy egrets, white ibises can be recognized by their reddish pink bills and legs as they forage among cypress and mangrove trees, using their down-curved bills to probe the mud for invertebrates.

Woodpeckers. Several species of woodpeckers call swamps home, including familiar downy, hairy and red-bellied varieties. One special swamp resident is the pileated woodpecker. Nearly as large as crows, these striking birds require big trees for their rectangular-shaped nest cavities and often set up shop in swampy areas.

163

THE WONDER OF WATER

▼ WOOD STORKS

Wood storks are picky waders. They need the water to be just right— not too deep and not too shallow. While swamp waters tend to be stained the color of tea, they aren't muddy or murky, which means that fish-eating birds like the wood stork can easily spot and scoop up a meal in the slowly flowing currents.

Warblers. After woodpeckers have hammered out holes in the sides of trees, sunny yellow warblers with blue wings take up residence in the woodpeckers' excavated apartments. These prothonotary warblers also nest in bird boxes. Found in eastern swamps from central Florida to southern Minnesota, they use boxes placed 4 to 12 feet high that look out over the water.

ROLAND JORDAHL

MADE TO WADE: THE GREAT BLUE HERON

Spotting a great blue heron always feels like a treat. Get ready to take a closer look into this statuesque waterbird's special qualities, behaviors and habitat.

◄ IN THE NEST

Great blue heron nests vary widely. A first-year nest may be only 20 inches across. Others, used repeatedly for many years, can reach 4 feet in diameter and be nearly as deep.

Despite their height (adults are around 4 feet tall), great blue herons typically weigh only 5 to 6 pounds, thanks to their light, hollow bones.

Males and females of this species look almost exactly alike. On average, males are a little larger, with longer ornamental plumes, but the distinctions are hard to make out, even when members of a pair are together.

Great blue herons are the largest and most widespread of all herons. They're usually seen alone unless they're near nesting colonies. A great blue heron colony might have more than 500 nests.

One part of the great blue heron that's less beautiful than the rest is its call. The rough squawk has a guttural, almost prehistoric sound.

For such large and lanky birds, herons are speedy, flying as fast as 30 mph. They usually fly with their necks in an S-shape and their legs trailing behind them.

In the winter, these birds fly south from snowy areas; their primary diet is fish, so if they can't feed from frozen lakes and streams, they have to go where the water is open until spring.

MARIE READ

◀ **EYES**
High-density light receptors in their eyes, called rods, allow great blue herons to hunt day or night.

▲ **BEAK**
A pointed beak is used to strike at or pick up food.

◀ **NECK**
An S-shaped neck works like a spring to strike quickly.

▶ **LEGS**
Long legs keep the majority of the body feathers dry while the bird stands in deep water or mud.

▼ **TOES**
Spread-out toes function as snowshoes to keep the bird from sinking into muck.

12 THINGS YOU DIDN'T KNOW ABOUT THUNDERSTORMS

Nothing captures the epic power of nature quite like a thunderstorm. Ponder these facts the next time the sky clouds over.

1 **Lightning strikes more** than 8 million times a day worldwide. That is about 93 times per second.

2 **Thunderstorms occur all** around the globe, but rarely over oceans or in the regions near the North and South poles.

3 **Just how hot** is a lightning bolt? About 50,000 degrees Fahrenheit—five times hotter than the surface of the sun.

4 **When a bolt** of lightning strikes sand, the sand heats up to very high temperatures. The melted sand resolidifies to form a glassy substance called fulgurite. The longest fulgurite specimen ever found, produced by a lightning flash in Florida in 1996, was nearly 16 feet in length.

5 **Hurricanes and typhoons** are actually the same type of event. What we call a hurricane in the United States is called a typhoon if it forms in the northwestern Pacific. Meteorologists also use the general term *tropical cyclone.*

6 **A typical thunderclap** has a sound pressure level of 120 decibels—about the same as a jet aircraft taking off nearby.

7 **You can be** struck by lightning even when it's not raining. About 10% of lightning strikes take place when there's no precipitation.

8 **The sound from** a lightning flash a mile away will take about five seconds to reach you. Counting the time interval between the flash and the bang is a handy way of estimating how far away that last lightning flash hit.

9 **The largest hailstone** ever recorded in the United States was found in July 2010 in Vivian, South Dakota. It was almost 19 inches around and weighed almost 2 pounds.

10 **It really can** rain frogs, fish and other unusual things. It's rare, but strong winds from a tornado or storm can be powerful enough to propel animals and objects high into the air (and they have to come down eventually).

11 **By one measure,** Tropical Storm Claudette was the wettest storm in U.S. history. It dumped 43 inches of rain in 24 hours—the most rain ever recorded in one day— on Alvin, Texas, in July 1979.

12 **Lightning can strike** the same place twice—and it often does, especially objects that are tall, pointy and isolated. The Empire State Building, for example, is hit almost 100 times a year, according to the CDC.

WEATHERING THE STORM

Learn how powerful hurricanes impact birds— and how you can help in the aftermath.

Sensing the storm. Birds don't have an early warning system for oncoming storms. Some scientists think birds might be able to detect the low-pitched rumbling of a distant hurricane—a sound that is too low for humans to hear—but there's no proof so far. Birds probably first notice a storm as winds increase gradually and bring scattered rain showers.

▶ SHOREBIRDS

Near the coast, a storm surge may drive marsh birds up and out of their habitat, putting them at great risk. Birds such as terns, plovers and black skimmers that nest on beaches and barrier islands are especially vulnerable to hurricanes early in the season. If a storm makes landfall before midsummer, many nests, eggs and young birds will be washed away.

JOHN GILL

Piping
plover

▲ SEABIRDS

When birds of the open ocean get caught in a hurricane's outer winds, they fly downwind until they end up in the calm eye at the storm's center. If a hurricane travels inland, it may bring along some of these birds—such as shearwaters and sooty terns—and eventually leave them deep in the continent's interior.

Migratory birds. Much like seabirds, migratory birds tend to concentrate in the eye of the storm as it moves toward land. After a storm, coastal areas may be carpeted with thousands of warblers, thrushes, and other migrants that have been carried back to shore. They will rest, feed and then continue their migration.

Backyard birds. Some large birds may fly away ahead of a storm, but most species will stay put and seek shelter. Woodpeckers may cling to the downwind sides of tree trunks or hide inside holes. Cardinals, buntings and other songbirds find spots deep in dense thickets, protected from the gales. Other backyard birds take cover under sheds or on the lee sides of houses.

Habitat destruction and recovery. Forests and marshes can take years to recover after a hurricane, but the results aren't always all bad. Sometimes a storm that knocks out a few trees will open up a forest and make it more diverse, allowing for more variety of bird life.

How to Help Birds After a Storm

If your area is impacted by a storm, consider taking a few of the following steps to assist your avian neighbors.

- Fill feeders with high-quality food such as suet cakes or sunflower seed.
- Offer water in a birdbath or other clean vessel.
- Check to see if licensed wildlife rehabilitators are operating after the storm. If you find an injured bird after the worst weather has passed, the rehab center may care for it, but keep in mind the center may be overwhelmed with other wildlife. If so, ask if they need donations or help.
- Volunteer to help restore habitat, such as coastal beaches.

A Drop of Magic

Birds begin to migrate through our area in summer and fall, and Cooper's and sharp-shinned hawks frequently visit our yard to "play" with the blue jays. This sharp-shinned stopped by one rainy day and parked on a tree in our yard. His posture in this picture reminds me of a magician. I can just imagine him saying: "And for my next trick ..."

—Don Whitehead
Duluth, Minnesota

DON WHITEHEAD

The Lowdown on Rainy-Day Bird Behavior

Experts Kenn and Kimberly Kaufman explain why birds stock up and sing out when stormy weather is nearby.

Q It seems that more birds than usual come to my feeder when it's raining. Why?
—*Jody Kreider*
Murrieta, California

KENN AND KIMBERLY: Wild birds pay close attention to the weather at all times, and with good reason—it has a huge impact on their survival. We often notice that birds feed more actively when storms are approaching. They may swarm the feeders, almost frantic to eat as much as possible, when a big blizzard is coming, but even a gentle rain seems to boost their appetites. Apparently they have an instinct to fill up when there's the threat of any kind of weather condition that may make food harder to find.

Q Why do birds sing after a storm?
—*Lori Sheldon*
Borger, Texas

KENN AND KIMBERLY: After a storm, especially a bad one, it's reassuring to hear birds singing. It's mostly male birds that sing. They tune up after storms for the same reasons they belt out songs early in the morning. Each male sings to announce his claim to a territory—the area that he defends for raising a family—and to communicate with his mate. So at dawn's first light, or as soon as the storm passes, the message in his song is "I'm still here." It reassures his mate that he's guarding the territory and lets neighboring males know that this turf is still occupied.

"The way I see it, if you want the rainbow, you gotta put up with the rain."

—DOLLY PARTON

LOU ANN

PLANTING A RAIN GARDEN

Start a rain garden to make better use of the water that nature provides.

Break ground. A rain garden should be 4 to 8 inches deep. The initial creation may require digging or even excavating, so be prepared for more than a day's work.

Know the benefits. A rain garden does much more than improve the beauty of your yard. It also provides habitat for wildlife such as birds and butterflies, reduces flooding, removes pollutants from stormwater and recharges groundwater.

Do the dirty work. Dig several inches of compost or other organic matter into the top 6 to 8 inches of soil before planting. This will improve drainage in heavy soils and increase the water retention of fast-draining soils.

Pick the right location. Plant rain gardens on a slight slope at least 10 feet from your home, and avoid planting them under mature trees. Established tree roots may make digging difficult and the additional moisture can be harmful to the tree.

Choose plants wisely. Select plants suited to temporary flooding and drought. Begin the process by looking at the native species in your area, then check with nature centers, extension offices and your state department of natural resources for more suggestions. As always, variety is key!

Size it right. A good size for an average rain garden is from 100 to 300 square feet. A garden that's about twice as long as it is wide, with the long end perpendicular to the sloping ground, best intercepts water runoff.

Enjoy the perks. After the first two years, native plants should be mature enough to outcompete any weeds, and the quick-filtering garden will prevent standing water, deterring mosquito activity.

10 RAIN GARDEN FAVORITES

Water-loving plants make a splash among birds, butterflies and bugs. These natives put spring showers to good use!

1 ◀ BLUE-EYED GRASS
Sisyrinchium angustifolium, **Zones 4 to 9.** This grasslike grower is actually a member of the iris family. Its violet-blue blooms appear in spring and make terrific cut flowers. Plant blue-eyed grass in full sun to partial shade and moist to wet soil for best results.

2 Blue Cardinal Flower
Lobelia siphilitica, **Zones 4 to 9.** Give this sun-loving perennial a bit of shade if your summers are very hot, and plant it in the wettest part of your rain garden. Spires of beautiful blue flowers appear in mid-to-late summer, attracting native bees, bumblebees and hummingbirds. Plus, it's deer resistant!

3 Turtlehead
Chelone glabra, **Zones 3 to 8.** Segue from summer into fall with these unique "turtle head"-shaped flowers. Spikes of pink-tinged white flowers top 2- to 3-foot-tall plants. Turtlehead is a pollinator magnet and a host plant for the Baltimore checkerspot butterfly caterpillar.

4 **Firedance Dogwood** *Cornus sericea* 'Firedance', Zones 2 to 7. This compact dogwood offers year-round charm and packs lots of beauty into its 3- to 4-foot size. White spring blossoms turn into white berries that attract birds. In fall, the leaves turn red-purple and drop to reveal red stems.

5 **Palm Branch Sedge** *Carex muskingumensis*, **Zones 4 to 9.** It's all about the foliage with this one. The glossy leaves glisten in the sun and pair well with other plants. When conditions are right, it creates a nice ground cover that weaves through nearby plants.

6 ▲ SWAMP ROSE MALLOW *Hibiscus moscheutos*, **Zones 4 to 9.** Flowers the size of dinner plates are sure to make visitors and passersby stop for a second look. This plant may start off slow in spring, but the showstopper can reach 3 to 7 feet tall. Mark its location to avoid weeding out this late-sprouting perennial.

7 Chokeberry
Aronia species,
Zones 3 to 9. Chokeberry has it all—spring flowers, glossy green leaves, vibrant red fall cover and winter fruit. The antioxidant-rich berries will make you pucker; even the birds leave them be until mid-to-late winter, when other food sources are scarce.

8 Swamp Milkweed
Asclepias incarnata,
Zones 3 to 6. Native to swamps and wet meadows, this hummingbird and butterfly magnet also tolerates dry soil. In mid-to-late summer, the plants are topped with fragrant, showy pink-to-mauve flowers. Both monarch and queen butterfly caterpillars like to munch on the leaves, while deer tend to leave it be.

9 Winterberry
Ilex verticillata, **Zones 3 to 9.** Light up your fall and winter rain garden with this deciduous holly. The bright red berries take center stage as the leaves drop in fall. Combine the berry-laden stems with evergreens to create an outdoor winter container (away from pets and children).

10 ▼ BUTTONBUSH
Cephalanthus occidentalis,
Zones 4 to 9. Add fragrance and seasonal beauty to sunny rain gardens with this native shrub. Butterflies, hummingbirds and bees will stop at the flowers in early summer; later, round fruits replace the flowers and persist into winter. Compact varieties such as Sugar Shack (3 to 4 feet tall) make buttonbush suitable for many landscapes.

WATER-WISE TIPS AND TRICKS

Take these easy steps to reduce outdoor water usage and keep your plants thriving.

Choose drought-tolerant plants. Some plants get all the water they need from rain, so once established, they require less attention.

Give your plants a solid soak. While sprinklers work, a soaker hose is better. It applies the water directly to the soil by the roots, so up to 90% of the water is actually available to plants.

◀ **HARVEST THE RAIN**
Place a rain barrel at your downspouts. A 1,000-square-foot roof collects about 625 gallons of water from just 1 inch of rain.

Supplement your soil. Adding organic matter such as compost, chopped-up leaves or composted manure to your soil will increase its water-holding capacity. A good rule of thumb is to add 1 inch of compost per year.

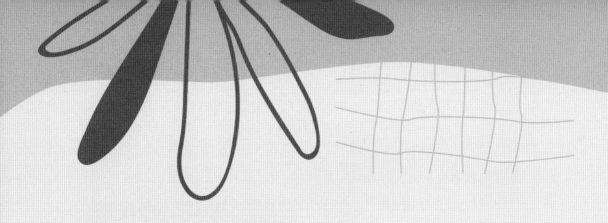

Reader Secrets: Don't Touch That Tap

Our community has a few inventive ways to keep plants happy without turning on the spigot.

When I fill the kiddie pool for my grandchildren, I don't dump it out after. Instead, I fill all my watering cans and buckets with the leftover water.

> —*Kathleen Norton*
> *Westminster, Massachusetts*

I have three rain barrels that I use all spring and summer to water my ornamental garden plants, to fill the birdbaths and fountains, and sometimes even to wash my hair!

> —*Anita Allen*
> *Tiro, Ohio*

I sprinkle each plant individually and deeply instead of mass drenching my gardens to save water.

> —*Charlotte Estabrook*
> *Signal Mountain, Tennessee*

I haven't hooked up my garden hose for years. Instead, I catch excess water with a bucket in my shower, capture condensation from my air conditioner and save water from when I wash produce.

> —*Lois Brumfield*
> *Portland, Oregon*

Letting my garden dry out during the day and then soaking the soil in the evening reduces evaporation.

> —*Ken Orich*
> *Lethbridge, Alberta*

Recycled water from a dehumidifier helps me water my plants.

> —*Nikki Conell*
> *Willoughby, Ohio*

DUCK SEASON(S)

They're everywhere, yet we tend to overlook them. What do ducks do all year?

Many bird-watchers don't spend a lot of time looking at ducks. Yet regularly seen in North America are more than 35 species, many of them with beautiful plumage and unique adaptations. Ducks are also unique among birds in their annual schedule. Here's a season-by-season look at what they get up to in a given year.

▶ SPRING

Bonded pairs migrate together in the spring, with the male following the female to the area where she previously hatched or nested. Once the female picks a spot, she'll lay one egg per day, usually in the morning. She doesn't sit on them until the clutch of about 9 to 11 eggs is nearly complete. About 25 days later, the ducklings all hatch within about 24 hours of each other.

Female ducks often replace some of their body feathers in early spring for extra camouflage on the nest. Their bills also fade to a drabber color so they are less likely to be spotted by a nearby predator.

Wood duck

Summer. The male leaves the female when she is partway through incubation and takes off on a molt migration. Some males will travel 500 miles to find a spot where they can replace feathers that have worn out from exposure to sun, wind, rain and sand. While molting, they are flightless for about a month. At this time of year, the males take on "eclipse plumage," losing their brightly colored feathers so predators can't see them during their flightless period.

▼ FALL

By midfall, drakes are looking dapper again, and they're already thinking about finding their mates for the next year. The spring ducklings, now full-size adults, are ready to take off on their first migration south—without their parents. Within only a few months of hatching, most species have handsome feathers and enter the arena to compete for a mate. As temperatures drop, they begin pushing south in groups, looking for open water to feed and roost.

CLIVE DODD/ALAMY STOCK PHOTO

Northern pintails

Winter. Winter marks the start of duck courtship rituals. Most species form their pair bonds between November and March, much earlier than most songbirds. Males put on colorful displays and elaborate dances, and all members of the same species perform the same display. If you see mallards pumping their heads in sync, it's a sign they are mates getting geared up to breed in the spring.

Divers vs. Dabblers

Within the duck family, there are two different groups. Here's what you need to know to tell them apart.

DABBLERS

Dabblers, including mallards and gadwalls, are the ducks you're most likely to see in shallow park ponds. To feed, these ducks pick at the water's surface or walk on land. Comblike structures on their bills help them sift tasty morsels from the water.

DIVERS

Divers are found in slightly deeper water. These species plunge underwater to snatch mussels, fish and submerged aquatic vegetation. Some divers have strong, thick-based bills ideal for prying mussels off rocks, while others have saw-toothed bills great for fishing. Large feet help them swim underwater but make them awkward on land.

THAT'S NOT A DUCK

If it looks like a duck and acts like a duck, then it must be a duck, right? Think again. Let's take a look at some duck doppelgängers to set the record straight.

◄ DOUBLE-CRESTED CORMORANT

Like the mergansers they resemble, double-crested cormorants are fish eaters. But unlike mergansers, cormorants aren't ducks. While you might see them swimming low in the water, you are just as likely to spot one basking in the sun with its wings spread wide. They don't have nearly as much preening oil as ducks, so cormorants air-dry their feathers.

Pied-billed grebe. These birds let out wailing *whoop*s and *kuh*s, but they don't quack. Grebes' legs are back on the body, making walking difficult. The birds will often dive rather than fly off when they feel threatened. Grebes can even adjust their buoyancy and sink down, swimming with their heads sticking up like periscopes.

▼ COMMON LOON

The common loon has a haunting, almost yodel-like sound, which echoes across northern lakes in the summer. Males and females have the same beautiful summer colors, which include a dark red eye, a jet-black head, and a bold black-and-white pattern across the back and chest. While loons do have a ducklike shape, their bills are long and sharp, perfect for fishing.

Common gallinule. This bird is especially prevalent in the southern coastal U.S. Look for the noticeable red bill and frontal shield on adult birds. Gallinules can resemble ducks when they are swimming, but they also have an impressive habit of walking on water (or rather, walking on floating vegetation), which showcases their huge feet and remarkably long toes.

▶ AMERICAN COOT

American coots are related to the rails. If you get a good look at this black water bird, notice the white, chickenlike bill and frontal shield. They also have partially lobed toes, not webbed feet like ducks. Coots are often seen swimming together in large numbers. Hesitant to take flight, they tend to flap frantically as they scurry along the water's surface.

Whistling-duck. Sure, they have *duck* in their name, but both black-bellied and fulvous whistling-ducks are more closely related to swans and geese than to true ducks. Look for them in southern states, especially Arizona, Texas and Florida. Male and female whistling-ducks look the same, and both help raise the whistling-ducklings.

Eared grebe. During the breeding season, an eared grebe sports yellow tufts of feathers along the sides of its head. In nonbreeding plumage, these birds are slate gray with accents of black and white. Like other grebes, the eared grebe chicks will ride atop the backs of their parents and can even remain in place as the adults dive underwater.

6 POND-EROUS MYTHS

*Forget what you've heard about water gardens—
the objections have been swept away with the
algae that spawned them.*

MYTH:

Small features are less work.

REALITY:

Large, mature water gardens are
easier to maintain. Smaller water
features rarely have the flow
or capacity necessary for long-
term stability and thus typically
require more maintenance.

MYTH:

**Maintaining a water garden is
a constant headache.**

REALITY:

Ecologically balanced water gardens let
Mother Nature do the work. In fact, a
well-designed, eco-friendly pond needs
only a biweekly removal of large debris
and an annual cleanout in cold climates.

MYTH:

Algae is always bad.

REALITY:

Some types of algae are a natural and beneficial part of a water garden's ecosystem. They lend a pleasing patina to rocks and a natural color to the water, and they provide food and oxygen for aquatic life. Excessive algae is usually a result of too much sunlight, so natural ponds should include aquatic plants that shade 50% of the pond's surface.

MYTH:

To keep fish, water gardens need to be deep.

REALITY:

Fish, including koi, can hibernate through the coldest winters in ponds just 2 feet deep. But be sure not to overpopulate your pond, which can lead to poor water quality and sick fish. Never exceed 1 inch of fish for every square foot of pond surface area.

MYTH:

Predators will eat your fish.

REALITY:

Koi are at risk mainly from great blue herons or raccoons. A motion-activated scarecrow system will deter these anglers with a spray of water. You can also install underwater tunnels or other hiding spots for your fish. Raccoons don't care to swim for their supper, so a pond that's at least 8 feet wide will keep them away from the deepest part of the water garden.

MYTH:

Water gardens are breeding grounds for mosquitoes.

REALITY:

A well-designed water garden has lots of flowing water, which will inhibit mosquito breeding (they breed in still, standing water). Ponds also support fish, frogs, toads and other wildlife that eat mosquito larvae.

Red-eyed
vireo

JUST ADD WATER

These feathered friends usually skip stocked feeders, but you can still attract them with fresh water.

◀ VIREOS

The birds in this musical group are noted for their near-constant singing from the treetops. A thicker bill helps distinguish them from other insect eaters. A simple water dish might not be enough to attract vireos, so consider a flowing fountain instead.

Wrens. House, Pacific and winter wrens hop and crawl through thickets as they forage. Look for the perky behavior and striped eyebrows of Carolina wrens in the East and Bewick's wrens in the West. Place birdbaths where you can see them to maximize your enjoyment of these birds.

Thrushes. American robins are the most familiar of these hefty, long-legged songbirds. As insect and berry specialists, thrushes are not particularly drawn to feeders, but they will slurp up water from a birdbath.

Waxwings. Both cedar and Bohemian waxwings are berry lovers. They travel in flocks, so sheltered perching locations and fruit-producing trees and shrubs attract these elegant visitors. After they enjoy a meal in a tree, they may be enticed closer to the ground with a water feature.

Golden-crowned kinglet

◄ KINGLETS

Tiny, active ruby-crowned and golden-crowned kinglets get their energy from scarfing insects high in the trees. Moving water may bring them down from the canopy, but after a brief refresh session at the water, they will quickly depart.

▲ TANAGERS

Western, scarlet and summer tanagers are some of
the most tropical-looking species that appear in the
United States and Canada, but they tend to stay up
in the treetops. Providing water can lure them down.

Bluebirds. While bluebirds are members of the thrush family, they're special enough to merit their own category. They may take mealworms from a feeder, but a birdbath is far more attractive to them—especially during cold snaps. Bluebirds can't eat snow, so set up a heated birdbath to keep water available to them year-round.

▼ THRASHERS

Providing shelter is key if you want to attract thicket-dwelling thrashers. Entice them by situating a birdbath near cover. Access to trees and shrubs protects songbirds from predators, and wet birds cannot fly well, so they need a place to preen themselves and stay safe.

Brown thrasher

Hummingbirds. Although hummingbirds get most of their hydration needs from all the sugar water and nectar they slurp up, they like to clean their feathers by flying through or sitting under the gentle spray of a moving water feature.

Keep Hummers Happy

Hummingbirds rinse off in the rain, at splashing streams or in the spray of waterfalls. Here's how to re-create in your own backyard the showers they love.

To set up an inexpensive solar fountain, you'll need a basin deep enough to submerge a small pump (or hold a floating model) and wide enough to catch and recycle the falling spray. A classic pedestal birdbath can work, but it may be too deep for hummingbirds. Add stones if needed to keep the water shallow.

Be sure to keep the small solar panel, attached to the pump by a cord, in direct sunlight. Maintenance is fairly simple—keep an eye on the water level, especially on windy days, and refill the basin as needed to ensure that the pump doesn't run dry.

Amp things up by adding a tiny perch. Choose a slim branching stick (about 4 feet long) with twigs skinny enough for tiny feet to grasp, and anchor the bottom of the stick by pushing it into the soil beside the basin. Then just sit back and enjoy the hummingbirds zipping through and preening in your backyard showers.

ID THAT AMPHIBIAN

Follow these key clues to spot the differences between frogs and toads.

Frog

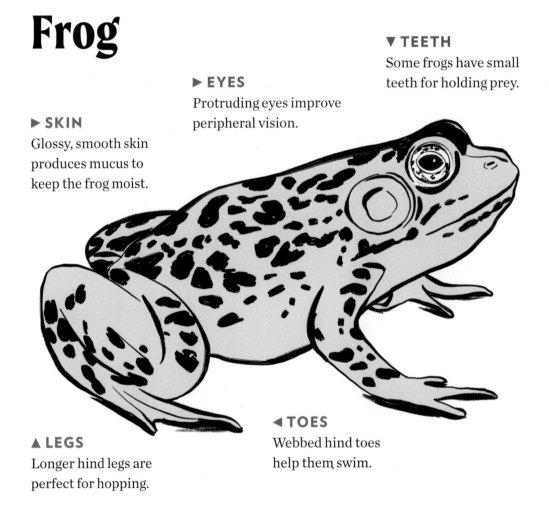

▶ SKIN
Glossy, smooth skin produces mucus to keep the frog moist.

▶ EYES
Protruding eyes improve peripheral vision.

▼ TEETH
Some frogs have small teeth for holding prey.

▲ LEGS
Longer hind legs are perfect for hopping.

◀ TOES
Webbed hind toes help them swim.

If it seems tough to tell a toad from a frog, there's a reason why! Toads are actually a subclassification of frogs—so, technically, these bumpy-skinned amphibians are frogs too. Both fall under the Anura order, meaning "without a tail," and both creatures are found on every continent except for Antarctica.

Toad

▼ EYES
Glands behind the eyes secrete poison to discourage predators.

▼ COLOR
Earthy (usually brown) coloring allows them to blend in on the ground.

◀ SKIN
Drier, thicker skin has bumps.

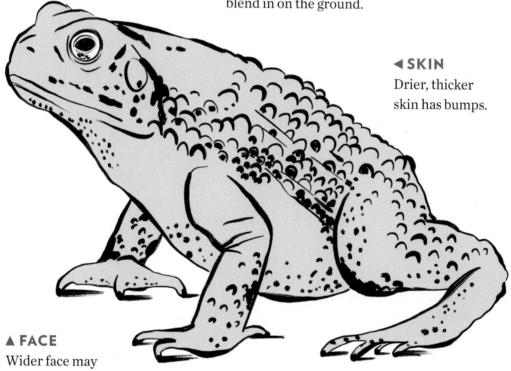

▲ FACE
Wider face may balloon to appear even bigger when threatened.

▲ LEGS
Stout legs are used for crawling more than leaping.

PUDDLE JUMPING

There's a surprising reason why butterflies flutter so quickly to a bit of standing water.

Little
yellows

BRYAN REYNOLDS

Most of us are used to seeing backyard butterflies flutter and dip between blooms in bright sunny gardens. But if you've ever seen butterflies gathering somewhere unexpected, like around mud puddles or the sandy banks of a river, you've actually been witness to a fascinating butterfly behavior known as puddling.

"Male butterflies, just like any living creature, are trying to ensure they reproduce," explains Ryan Fessenden of the Florida Museum of Natural History's Butterfly Rainforest. "One of the ways they do that is by passing on nutrients, along with genetic material, to the females when they are mating."

When butterflies mate, the males transfer a spermatophore to the females. Think of this as a tiny package that holds just about everything a female needs to produce healthy fertilized eggs. Part of the package includes nutrients that help support the female butterfly's health, making her offspring more likely to survive.

"Male butterflies gather those nutrients by drinking water from wet spots on the ground, collecting various

minerals and nutrients such as sodium and amino acids," Ryan says.

And it's not just the mud that attracts butterflies. Like other animals, butterflies need salt in their diet, and they find it in some very unexpected spots, such as in crocodile tears or human sweat. They're also drawn to less savory items such as decaying flesh, excrement and even blood.

Off-putting as it may seem, these behaviors are vital to their survival.

That's why you may see huge swarms of dozens or even hundreds of butterflies when a good puddling spot appears. "The more males that can gather nutrients, the more success the species will have reproducing," Ryan says. "So when a wet spot or puddle is found by one, other butterflies will notice and join in." They are all there for one reason— to ensure they survive and thrive for many generations to come.

Pipevine and eastern tiger swallowtails

Create a Puddling Station

Help butterflies, especially during dry weather, with a DIY puddling spot.

- Find and fill a shallow dish or container with soil or sand. Add a few flat rocks to provide perching spots.
- Pour enough water in the container to moisten the soil, and sprinkle some salt on the surface. Also set out overripe fruit such as bananas and oranges.
- Keep the soil moist during the heat of the day, when butterflies are more likely to visit.

Who's Thirsty?

When it comes to identifying puddling butterflies, it's helpful to know the usual suspects.

Any type of butterfly can puddle, but it's most common in members of the swallowtail family, sulphurs and whites. In particular, look for tiger swallowtails, red-spotted purples, white admirals, cabbage whites, and clouded and cloudless sulphurs at puddles.

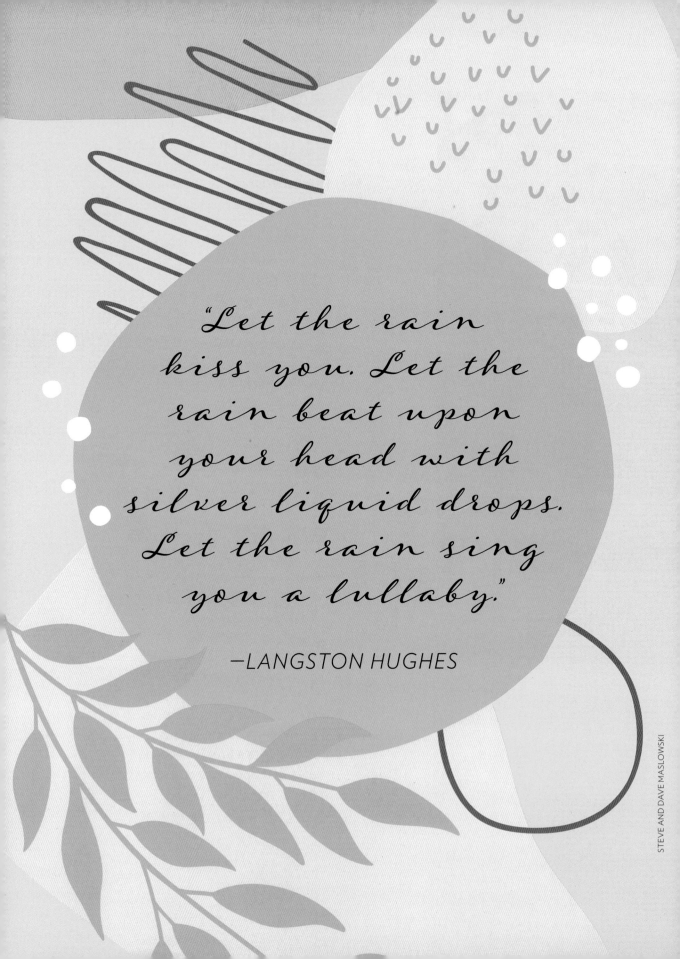

"Let the rain kiss you. Let the rain beat upon your head with silver liquid drops. Let the rain sing you a lullaby."

—LANGSTON HUGHES

STEVE AND DAVE MASLOWSKI

A Deeper Green

PLANTING A LOVE OF NATURE YIELDS LIFTED SPIRITS, STRONG COMMUNITIES, HEALTHY WILDLIFE AND A HAPPY PLANET.

We all have favorite species, memories, gardening rituals and more that make our bonds with nature feel deeply personal. But when we pursue the threads tying those passions to the wider world, our minds, bodies, neighborhoods and ecosystems become richer and more alive. Step into the fresh air, take a deep breath and discover why the grass is always greener on nature's side.

A HEALTHY DOSE OF NATURE

Nature lovers have long touted the healing benefits of getting outside. The conclusions of these scientific studies seal the deal.

◄ THINK OUTSIDE THE BOX

Nature helps us solve problems. A 2014 study from Stanford University found that walking boosted participants' creativity by 60% on average, with the best ideas coming during strolls in green spaces.

A few minutes in the great outdoors can do wonders for our concentration. A 2008 study showed that a 20-minute walk in a park had attention-boosting effects that could rival those of prescription stimulants.

Even the smell of the outdoors is calming: A 2009 Japanese study found that inhaling phytoncides, chemicals produced by trees, causes levels of stress hormones to drop.

According to American and Taiwanese researchers, workers near a window sleep an average of 46 minutes more per night than their windowless peers.

▼ TAKE A FOREST BATH

In Japan, *shinrin-yoku*—literally "forest bathing," but essentially spending time in the woods—has been linked to everything from lower blood pressure and pulse rate to higher activity of anti-cancer proteins.

Nature's benefits stick with us. Tokyo researchers measured "natural killer cells" in healthy women before and after three walks through forests. Spiked levels of these cancer-fighting cells lasted more than a week after exposure to forest air.

Living near nature curbs loneliness. A 2009 study of 10,089 Dutch residents found that having green spaces close to their homes promoted a sense of community and stronger feelings of social support.

A 2001 University of Washington study found that after eight weeks of walking outdoors for 20 minutes daily, women aged 19 to 78 reported increased self-esteem and fewer signs of depression.

A landmark study conducted in 1984 at a Pennsylvania hospital found that rooms with a view of the outdoors can lower recovery time and reduce pain and depression.

We live longer when we're closer to nature. Japanese academics tracked 3,144 senior citizens in Tokyo over five years. Those living near walkable green spaces were significantly more likely to be alive at the end of the study.

Nature can calm an overloaded brain. Researchers at two Edinburgh universities monitored a dozen healthy adults who walked through a shopping district, a busy commercial strip and a park. Their brainwaves became more reflective and less frustrated during the green stroll.

In 2001, academics found that in Chicago social-housing communities, proximity to nature was linked to reduced aggression and fear, as well as better self-discipline. The greener the buildings' surroundings, the fewer crimes reported there.

Feeling burnt out at work? Having plants at the office is associated with fewer sick days and greater productivity.

THE BACKYARD LABORATORY

Ready to join the citizen science movement and help researchers learn more about nature? Here are nine projects you can contribute to right from your own backyard.

eBird. EBird is the ultimate citizen science project for birders. More than 100 million bird spottings are reported to eBird every year, and it's become the No. 1 place to go for information on birding hot spots, tracking and more. *ebird.org*

Project FeederWatch. Each winter, birders join FeederWatch to record sightings at their backyard feeders. Even common birds, such as blue jays and cardinals, help scientists understand the health of ecosystems and the impacts of climate change. *feederwatch.org*

▶ MONARCH LARVA MONITORING PROJECT

The monarch butterfly is instantly recognizable, and many people know the migratory population is struggling. Breeding monarchs are the subject of this program. Participants report regularly on eggs, caterpillars and milkweed, which the fliers need to survive. *monarchjointventure.org/mlmp*

Great Backyard Bird Count. Anyone anywhere can join in the GBBC, which takes place over four days every February. Participating is as easy as watching the birds that visit your backyard and reporting them to the website. *birdcount.org*

Project NestWatch. If winter is for watching feeders, spring is for watching nests. NestWatchers monitor nesting birds, tracking their outcomes and exploring trends such as timing, number of eggs, success rate and more. *nestwatch.org*

Project Noah. Project Noah aims to document all of Earth's living organisms. Upload your sightings, even if you haven't been able to identify them, and members of the Project Noah community offer ID suggestions. It's possible to spend hours browsing sightings from around the globe—and helping others identify their findings. *projectnoah.org*

▼ EBUTTERFLY

EButterfly aims to be for butterflies what eBird is for birds. It's a place to document your sightings, keep track of your butterfly life list, upload and share photos, and more. *e-butterfly.org*

Project Budburst. Project Budburst studies phenology in plants. Participants monitor and report on the timing of major events in plant life cycles, including flowering, leafing and fruiting. The findings help scientists understand the wider effects of climate change and extreme weather events. *budburst.org*

OPT OUTSIDE

Some "big years" go far beyond birding! Enjoy the great outdoors with these 12 fresh-air adventures.

January. Ask your local Audubon chapter or neighborhood nature center for a list of events, classes and field trips, and sign up for something that intrigues you. Programs are often free—and you'll meet other nature lovers.

▶ **FEBRUARY**
If you live somewhere that gets a lot of snow, make the most of the flurries and try your hand at a cold-weather sport such as skiing, snowshoeing or ice-skating. And if you're really looking for something new, try snowga, a combination of snowshoeing and yoga.

March. Early spring is the prime time to forage for delicious morel mushrooms, which boast an earthy, trufflelike flavor. Because of their short growing season, morels are always in high demand, so get out there when the season arrives. The day after a rain, when temps are just above 60, is ideal. Note: Do your research first to avoid a poisonous look-alike.

Barn owl

▲ APRIL

Celebrate Earth Day on April 22 by giving back to Mother Nature. You could plant trees, pick up litter or monitor a nest box for the National Audubon Society. *Volunteermatch.org* can also help you discover the specific interests and needs of groups in your community.

May. Try geocaching. It's a large-scale scavenger hunt, and anyone with a GPS or smartphone can participate. Download the free app to get coordinates and clues to millions of geocaches around the world. Finding your first one is a real treat! Visit *geocaching.com* to get started.

June. If you're able, participate in National Great Outdoors Month by living in it. Think hiking, s'mores and stargazing. Camping is family-friendly, inexpensive and relaxing—and you don't have to travel far. Your own backyard can be a great place to begin.

July. Visit a national park and enjoy the picturesque sights, hiking trails, lakes, rivers and more. At federal parks, you can keep track of your visits with a special passport, getting a stamp for each site as a way to remember the adventure. Visit *nps.gov/findapark* and choose your first stop.

August. Volunteer at a local farm, beekeeper or CSA to learn what farming is like. Connect with growers at farmers markets or by visiting *localharvest.org*. Another resource, *wwoof.net* (Worldwide Opportunities on Organic Farms), connects volunteers with organic farmers to promote cultural and educational opportunities.

September. A crisp fall morning is a wonderful time to head outside and practice some nature photography. Changing leaves form a perfect backdrop for migrating birds that visit backyard feeders; set up a few dead tree branches in the garden to provide extra perches for them and to increase your odds of capturing the perfect shot.

October. Fall harvest season is an excellent time to explore orchards and farms with your family and friends. Get lost in your state's best corn maze, find the funkiest pumpkin in the field and gather enough apples at the orchard to make a pie.

November. Go birding with friends. You can stay local or gather a group for a fall migration road trip. Check out Cape May, New Jersey, for an all-around birding spot, or find a desert oasis for waterfowl, cranes and geese at Bosque del Apache National Wildlife Refuge in New Mexico.

December. Branch out from your patio perch and connect with tens of thousands of birders across the country in the Christmas Bird Count, which runs from Dec. 14 to Jan. 5 each year. Visit *Audubon.org/Christmas-bird-count* for more details, then count your finds with fellow enthusiasts.

Praying
mantis on
coneflower

GROW A CHEMICAL-FREE GARDEN

A more natural approach can protect backyard plants and wildlife, as well as pets, children and neighbors. Making the switch is easier than you think.

◀ RECOGNIZE ALLIES

Less than 1% of the pest population of a garden can truly be considered pests. Most of these bugs are actually your garden allies, ready to take on the bad bugs. The good guys include pollinators (bees, butterflies, moths), parasitic wasps and parasitoids (wasps, ants, sawflies), and predators (birds, spiders, praying mantises, dragonflies).

Protect your garden ecosystem.
Pesticides, fungicides and herbicides don't just kill pests and weeds—they also kill helpful birds and insects. According to the National Audubon Society, an estimated 7 million birds die each year because of exposure to lawn pesticides.

Bug hotel

Protect your community.
Pesticides can pollute the runoff water that flows into our water systems, and some lawn pesticides contain carcinogens, which are linked to birth defects and nervous system, liver and kidney damage. At a minimum, they should be kept away from children and pets.

Consider less-toxic alternatives.
Insecticidal soaps or horticultural oils can help control aphids, flies, crickets and mites, but don't use them if bees are present. To deter slugs, scatter coffee grounds around your plants. Irish spring soap deters rabbits or deer. Cayenne pepper works for other critters.

Nurture healthy plants. The first line of defense in a pesticide-free garden is healthy plants. Choose native, disease-resistant plants that fit the growing conditions, and load up your soil with compost and organic matter. Organic mulch will protect your soil and provide a habitat for beneficial predators such as ground beetles, centipedes and spiders.

◀ GARDEN WITH INSECTS IN MIND

Choose colorful, flowering plants to attract bees and parasitoid wasps. Grow a variety of plants at different sizes, and don't be too tidy—a more natural garden can provide shelter and nesting spots for beneficial bugs (as well as your favorite birds). Installing a bug hotel can also encourage valuable pest-eating insects to stay in your yard.

Help your houseplants too. If you spot any insects on indoor plants, first wrap the pot in a garbage bag (to avoid washing potting mix down the drain) and give the plant a quick rinse. Follow with organic insecticides as needed. To fight whiteflies, enlist yellow sticky traps. For fungus gnats, sprinkle bits of Mosquito Dunks on the soil surface and water them in.

Plants That Beneficial Insects Love

These plants will draw in some of nature's best exterminators.

1. Creeping thyme
2. Marjoram
3. Tarragon
4. Rosemary
5. Lavender
6. Mexican sunflower
7. Dill
8. Oregano
9. Fennel
10. Salvia
11. Sage
12. Yarrow
13. Mint
14. Catmint

KEEP OUT SPACE INVADERS

Invasive plants decrease habitat diversity and water quality, increase soil erosion, and crowd out natives that support local birds and bugs. These pointers can help you weed out invaders for good.

Be methodical. Taking a systematic approach can make removing invasives easier. First, identify any harmful species in your yard. Research the best removal methods and then destroy small infestations. For larger problems, start with the property borders to stop the spread before tackling the epicenter.

▼ GET RID OF TICK HAVENS

Removing invasive plants can help reduce disease-carrying tick populations. Studies have found that Japanese barberry and honeysuckle bushes create the perfect habitat for both deer and the ticks that feed on them.

Japanese honeysuckle

▶ SHOP SMARTER

Most invasive plants are labeled as low-maintenance wonders, such as Eurasian honeysuckle and kudzu, or blooming beauties, such as Dame's rocket. Before planting, check with your university extension service, local nature center or state department of natural resources to be sure a new plant is not prohibited and can be grown in your area.

Pay attention to decor. Door swags and wreaths often contain invasive plants such as teasel and oriental bittersweet. Their seeds can spread from the arrangements into nearby gardens, eventually making their way to natural spaces.

Kudzu

Spread the word. Talk to your neighbors about the negative impact of invasives and encourage them to replace problem plants. If everyone works together, invasive seed sources will dwindle and you all will experience greater success.

Enjoy the rewards. You may find wildflowers filling your woods after removing buckthorn, honeysuckle and garlic mustard. Some people even uncover cherished heirloom plants once hidden by overgrowth. You never know what will pop up!

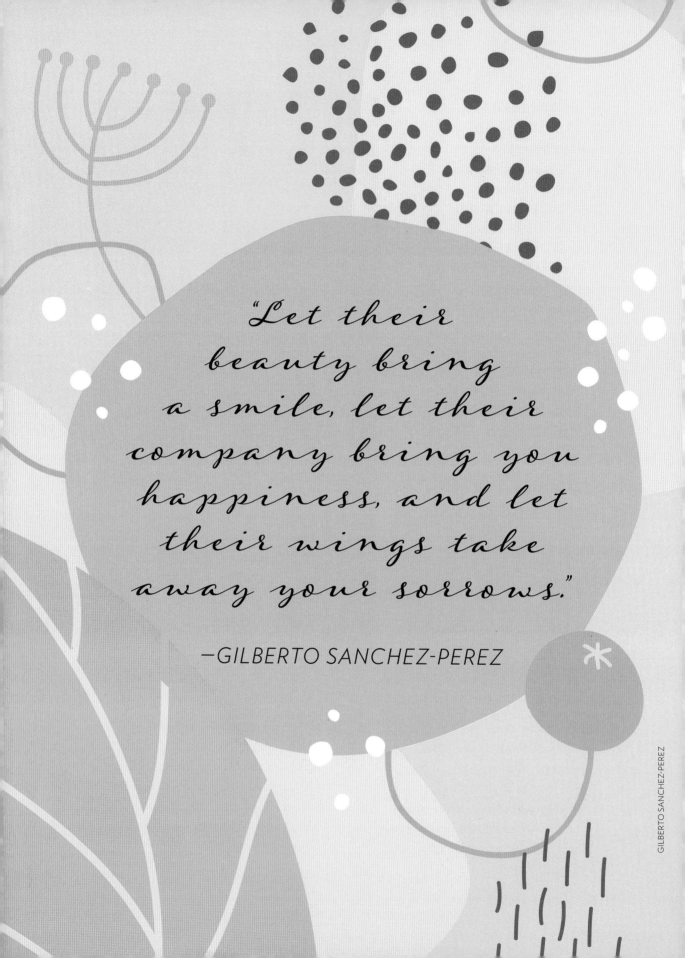

"Let their beauty bring a smile, let their company bring you happiness, and let their wings take away your sorrows."

—GILBERTO SANCHEZ-PEREZ

Broad-billed
hummingbird
at Mexican
flame bush

MEET YOUR VEGETABLES

CSAs help people form connections with local farmers—and fresh produce. Here's what to know before signing up and digging in.

What is it? In short, a CSA (Community Supported Agriculture) program is a way for consumers to buy food directly from local farmers. Members buy a "share" of the farm's yield in advance, and then they generally receive a weekly box of fresh produce during harvest season.

Can I participate? Due to an increasing interest in eating locally and sustainably raised food, chances are there's a CSA program in your area. Visit *localharvest.org /csa* to search by ZIP code for one nearby.

Are there any rules? There will most likely be a cutoff date for joining, so sign up early and be prepared to pay the fee for the entire season up front. Each CSA has its own guidelines, so find out in advance what happens if you're on vacation, forget to pick up your share and so on. Don't be afraid to ask questions!

How do CSAs help farmers? Because members tend to pay for the full season ahead of time, farmers have cash to invest directly into their operations. And based on input from members, the farmers have a better sense of local demand and a guaranteed customer base. Plus, they have a chance to meet their buyers!

How do CSAs help members? CSAs are a great way to eat fresh, seasonal local produce even if you don't have space or time for a garden. You'll be supporting your community and getting more variety in your diet, and you'll know exactly where your food is coming from.

How will I use all the produce? It's true—you've got to love cooking with vegetables for a CSA to be worthwhile. Store your veggies properly as soon as they arrive, embrace new ingredients, and share with friends and neighbors. You can even join with a friend and swap your favorites. Finally, plan ahead: The season tends to start lighter than it finishes.

SECRETS FROM THE FARMERS MARKET

We asked farmers from all over the country to share their best ideas for enjoying local markets and getting to know vendors. Here are their top tips.

◄ STOCK UP

It's generally best to buy the most of whatever is in season. Not only will it be abundant, it will usually be a bargain.

Learn their schedules. Some vendors have their own roadside stands or will be at multiple locations during the week. Ask them where else you can find them. It's a good way to discover new places for fresh veggies.

Scrub 'em. The produce probably got rinsed before it appeared at the market, but you should still wash everything you buy before you cook or eat it.

Be adventurous. Many farmers will have heirloom varieties, which may look different from the picture-perfect tomatoes and carrots you're used to. Go to the market vowing to try at least one thing you don't typically buy.

Take notice. Look around for nonprofit or just plain offbeat booths that might be at the market. You might gain a whole new perspective on what's available in your community.

Compare and contrast. Not all markets are the same. Look for those that specialize in homegrown and home-crafted items.

Make friends. Get to know the farmers—ask for cards or write down their contact info. They are used to providing this information. Then you can get their products regularly, not just when the market is open.

Ask questions. Farmers love to talk about what they raise. They often take great pride in educating customers about their farms and their wares, and they'll usually be glad to offer storage tips, cooking suggestions and even gardening advice.

▼ BRING A TOTE

Stash a reusable bag in your car to reduce the number of plastic bags that farmers have to provide for sales. Of course, make sure the bag can hold plenty.

◀ LEARN ABOUT ORGANICS

If you care about how the vendors raise their produce, ask if their farm is certified organic. Though many will have a sign saying as much, don't hesitate to ask how the food was grown, what was used for fertilizer, and how pests and weeds are controlled.

Take good care. Don't leave fresh produce in a hot car. If you need to run errands after your market trip, bring a cooler for your goods.

Look around. You don't have to stop at the first stand you see that has artichokes. It's perfectly OK (and part of the experience) to walk the market first to compare prices and produce. Then you can decide where to spend your money.

Don't haggle. Haggle at a flea market, not the farmers market. Farmers are almost always giving you the best price they can while maintaining a profit margin. Be happy to pay in full—you're supporting a local farm.

Bring cash. Not all vendors will have access to electronic card readers to process debit or credit card transactions.

Go early. Head to the market right before it opens to scope out what's for sale. Then you can map your route—and make sure your favorite items don't sell out before you get to the stall.

Don't be grabby. Sure, you can inspect the fruit and veggies and help yourself, but don't handle every single tomato in your search.

COMMUNITY GARDEN DO'S AND DON'TS

Participating in a community garden allows you to connect with others while growing bundles of fresh produce. These pointers will help you make the most of your experience.

DO:

Make the most of your garden plot. Once you harvest your spring crops, use the space to plant more veggies for late summer or early fall.

DON'T:

Forget about your garden! It's easy to overlook because you don't see it every day, but make a schedule and check on it regularly.

DO:

Consider finding a community space with a friend. That way, if one of you is busy or goes on vacation, there's always someone available to tend to the garden.

DON'T:

Invade your neighbor's space. Many people use community gardens, so be careful to stick to your own plot.

DON'T:

Ignore weeds. They won't confine themselves to your plot, and your neighbors won't be happy.

DO:

Make new friends. Other gardeners might have excess cherry tomatoes, while you have more squash than you can use. Time to trade!

DO:

Branch out beyond tomatoes, peppers and cukes. Growing unique heirloom beans or bicolored eggplants could make you the talk of the garden. Be adventurous!

BIRD-WATCHING FOR HEART & SOUL

Birding can lift our spirits and enrich our lives. Here are just a few reasons why birding is so beloved—straight from the heart.

Because it builds confidence. Birding is not just a passion but a skill that can be honed and improved over time. As we continue spending time among the birds, their names come naturally to us and their songs ring increasingly familiar in our ears. We soon notice this confidence and mastery translating to other areas of our lives.

Because it keeps us humble. Even veteran birders have a lot to learn. Every day brings brand-new behaviors from birds we thought we knew, and every day we remember how much we have yet to discover. Each time we step out the door, there may be new species to spot, new patterns to identify, new calls to recognize—and the list goes on. The ability to say "I don't know" keeps a person open-minded and flexible, always ready to learn.

Because it's easy. Anywhere we go, some birds are easy to find and easy to recognize. If we need a healthy escape from the stress or complication of everyday life, we can quickly be absorbed in watching a cardinal, bluebird or great blue heron. After this kind of relaxation, we can come back refreshed and rejuvenated, ready to tackle the tasks of the day again.

Because it's a challenge. Some birds just don't want to be seen—we have to be on high alert to notice them at all. And it takes real effort to distinguish between types of native sparrows, flycatchers, fall warblers and female ducks. Learning to recognize new birds exercises our brains, and studying their behaviors stretches our imaginations, giving us more mental energy for everything else in our lives.

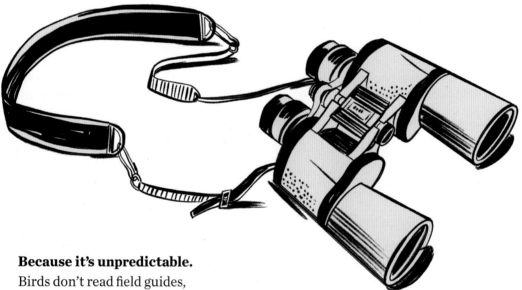

Because it's unpredictable. Birds don't read field guides, and they don't always follow the patterns we expect. Varied thrushes from the Pacific Northwest have landed in backyards all along the Atlantic coast. Green violet-ear hummingbirds from the tropics have visited feeders in Wisconsin. The exciting possibility of spotting something rare keeps us alert and alive to the wonders around us.

Because it's predictable. The annual cycles of bird behavior and migration give us something to look forward to and to count on for reassurance. These perennial reminders from nature's calendar help keep us grounded in the real world.

Eastern
bluebirds

Palm
warbler

Because birds are beautiful. At the end of the day, there's no denying it: Their colors, patterns, songs and graceful flight make birds some of the world's loveliest creatures. They motivate and inspire us, challenge and delight us. Birds enliven our imaginations. They're vibrant reminders of the amazing gifts the natural world has to offer to those who are aware and looking.

What the Science Says

The power of the natural world has long fascinated researchers and has led them to some impressive conclusions. Here are just a few:

- Researchers in Oregon found that outdoor recreational activities (such as hiking and canoeing) are associated with feelings of well-being, including life satisfaction. These findings held true regardless of age, gender, income, education level, fitness or knowledge of nature.

- A UK study found that people who live in neighborhoods with more afternoon bird populations report less stress, anxiety and feelings of depression.

- Researchers in Kentucky found that people who rested outdoors versus inside showed an increase in positive feelings and a decrease in tiredness. This means that simply watching a bird feeder outside for as little as 10 minutes can be beneficial to your psychological health.

Meeting the Neighbors

My neighbor grows sunflowers every year and opens up his fields to the community. People come from all over the county to take photos of the flowers. I love them, too, but I especially enjoy when a songbird like this indigo bunting perches on a flower head and poses for a portrait.

—*Donna Bourdon*
Ooltewah, Tennessee

How Do You Share Birding with Others?

Take some advice from these readers and spread your love of winged visitors.

Making custom birdhouses for wrens and chickadees started as a way to treat friends and family, and now I even sell a few. I built my 240th birdhouse this summer!

　　—Scott Gardner
　　Brandon, South Dakota

When I got into birding, I bought the *Birds of Pennsylvania Field Guide* by Stan Tekiela. I often give this book as a gift along with some seed.

　　—Bernice Manzoni
　　Monroe Township,
　　Pennsylvania

My community has a friendly competition to see who can spot the first oriole at their feeder. Some years we all see one on the same day!

　　—Stacy Stubbe
　　Ackley, Iowa

When I monitor nest boxes around the parks in my area, sometimes people ask what I'm doing. I let them know what I'm up to and occasionally give them a peek inside if the young have left.

　　—Dawn Cassel
　　Downingtown, Pennsylvania

I paint birds in watercolor, and then I make cards out of the paintings for special occasions.

　　—Joyceline Huennekens
　　Weaverville, North Carolina

I buy field guides at yard sales and give them to new birders.

　　—Mary Fox
　　Fair Grove, Missouri

PLANTING SUNSHINE

Kansas gardener Jennifer Broadstreet Hess shares how a successful new sunflower plot lifted her spirits during a pandemic.

I've always been in awe of the sprawling sunflower fields around my town in rural Marion County, Kansas. The wild sunflower is actually so common in Kansas that it's considered a weed—but it's also the state flower. And regardless of whether the fields are wild and filled with native Kansas species or boasting a farmer's crop of yellow abundance, the sight of these cheery flowers always makes my heart beat a little faster and puts a big smile on my face.

When the COVID-19 pandemic began in early 2020, I felt a bit sad and isolated—as did so many others— and I couldn't seem to shake the blues. Cultivating a wildflower plot and vegetable garden wasn't enough to distract me from the chain of ups and downs on the evening news, so I decided it was time to grow my own patch of sunshine.

I started by ordering a variety pack of sunflower seeds online. During the colder months I watched numerous YouTube videos on how to plant the seeds, so I felt a bit more prepared for the upcoming spring.

After picking a location I could view from my dining room window,

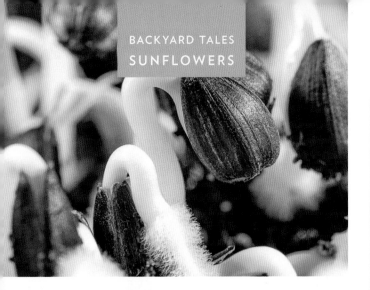

I was both excited and nervous. The ground around my property is full of limestone, making it difficult to work with, and the soil in the spot I chose was so poor that even grass never grew well there. To give my blooms a chance at success, I rototilled the top 2 feet of soil, pulled any weeds and mixed in a large bag of organic planting mix.

In late May, I carefully planted my seeds in trays using potting mix, and I left them to bask in the sun on my south-facing enclosed porch. They grew quickly from the intense heat and with a daily watering regimen. By mid June, they had sprouted and were finally ready to be planted in the ground.

I placed the sunflowers about 5 inches apart and made sure to water them each morning. Deep watering encourages sunflower roots to shoot downward, giving them a sturdy base. As they grew in height, I staked each corner of the plot and used garden wire at four different levels to further support the flowers against the Kansas winds. I eagerly logged their progress, marking about a foot of new growth every week.

By late July, a few of the stalks were over 5 feet tall and beginning to form buds. My sunflower patch was starting to come together with the broadening leaves of each plant. It took another two weeks for the blossoms to open.

About seven varieties of flowers bloomed in bright shades of light yellow, white and orange—some even displayed red hues! The vibrant pops of color awakened my spirit and lifted my mood as I went out to greet them each and every morning.

Planting and tending to these sunny showstoppers was one of the best and most rewarding learning experiences I've ever had in my garden. I can't wait to broaden the project this year and enjoy new bounties of blooms for many seasons to come.

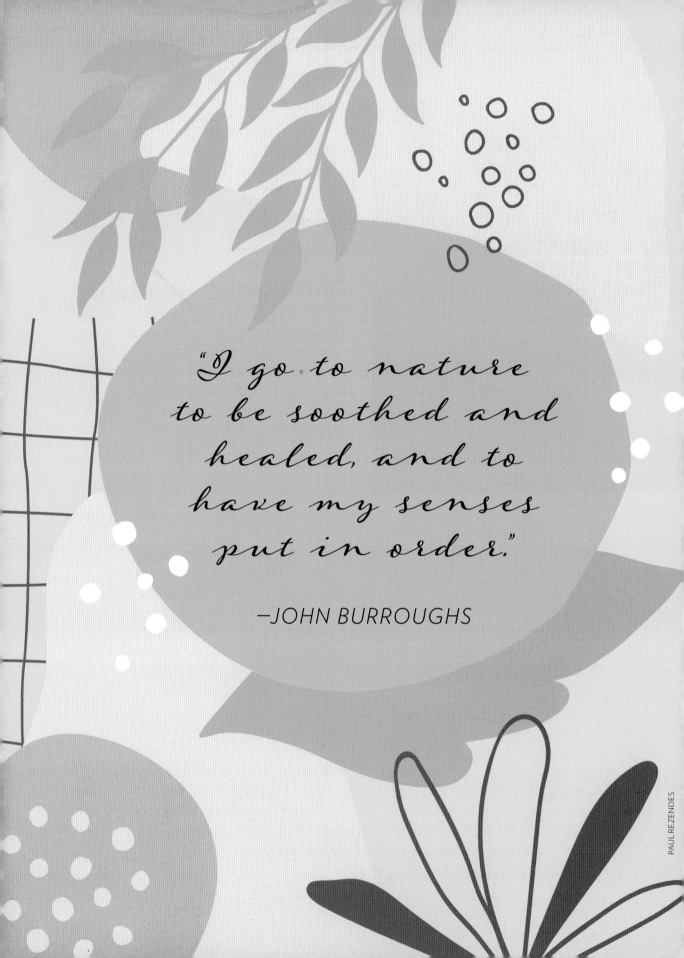

"I go to nature
to be soothed and
healed, and to
have my senses
put in order."

–JOHN BURROUGHS

PAUL REZENDES